ZEN ENCOUNTERS WITH LONELINESS

ZEN ENCOUNTERS *with* LONELINESS

Terrance Keenan

WISDOM PUBLICATIONS • BOSTON

Wisdom Publications
199 Elm Street
Somerville, MA 02144 USA
www.wisdompubs.org

Previously published as *St. Nadie in Winter: Zen Encounters with Loneliness*
(Boston: Journey Editions, 2001).

Library of Congress Cataloging-in-Publication Data
Keenan, Terrance, 1947–
 [St. Nadie in winter]
 Zen encounters with loneliness / by Terrance Keenan.
  p. cm.
 "Previously published as St. Nadie in Winter: Zen Encounters with Loneliness. (Boston: Journey Editions, 2001)."
 ISBN 1-61429-186-1 (pbk. : alk. paper)
 1. Keenan, Terrance, 1947– 2. Zen priests—United States—Biography. 3. Librarians—United States—Biography. 4. Spiritual biography—United States. I. Title.
 BQ968.K44A3 2014
 294.3'092—dc23
 [B]
                        2014008797
ISBN 9781614291862   eISBN 9781614292036

18 17 16 15 14
5 4 3 2 1

Cover and interior design by Gopa&Ted2, Inc.
Set in Janson Text 10.5/15.2.

Visit www.fscus.org.

For
Jane, Bryna, and Conor

CONTENTS

ACKNOWLEDGMENTS

I wish to thank my editor, Andy Francis, who was willing to take on a new edition of this book, for his always sensitive and mindful support throughout; my wife, Jane, for her meticulous reading and loving support; my son, Conor, for his moral support and deep insight; and my daughter, Bryna, for her open-hearted understanding. My gratitude goes also to my teachers, the Venerable Eido Shimano Roshi and the Venerable Roko Shinge Roshi, for permission to quote from their book, *Endless Vow: The Zen Path of Soen Nakagawa*, for their rigorous support of my practice, and for their profound teaching. May true Dharma continue.

A Note to the Reader

Many of the poems that appear throughout the prose portions of *Zen Encounters with Loneliness* were composed in concert with other poems and are meant to be read alongside of each other. All of the poems are presented together with their counterparts under the heading "Selected Poems" at the end of the book, so they may be read as they were intended to be.

INTRODUCTION

You're in my blood like holy wine.
You taste so bitter and so sweet.
—Joni Mitchell

Reality is the last nostalgia. We look upon it with hopeful sweetness, yet we grip it with the iron tenacity of desperation brought on by the terrifying accident of life. Purpose. Meaning. Certainty. Truth. Or perhaps the other view—Emptiness, Chaos, Doubt, Chance. However we seek to understand reality, whether through the scientific method, reason, religion, mysticism, philosophy, whatever perspective the conditions of our being compel us to use, we nevertheless wish reality to be so.

As one approaches the remote monastery Dai Bosatsu Zendo Kongo-ji, where I go for training, coming up the two mile long drive from the gatehouse through deep deciduous forest, just before one crosses the little plank bridge by the lake and sees the main buildings, there is the entrance to the Sangha Meadow, or cemetery. Here where deer browse lie the ashes of students of Buddhism. What did their study bring them? At the entrance there is a small Jizo Bodhisattva statue and a large stone slab. Cut into the stone is the calligraphic figure of 道 dō or "Way." Below this, much smaller, the words of a poem by Basho in English. I stood on foot before it, my first visit one autumn a decade ago, as my father lay dying in a state far away, remote from all my experience. What was I doing here? What were these fictions called memories? What did my father's death mean? What was his life? Was it real in any way that made sense? What was *my* life? Who was I, anyway? Leaves scattered across the dirt road and brushed the stone. These were Basho's words:

> Along this Way
> goes no one,
> this autumn evening.

No one. Me. I empty out. For a moment there are no questions and my sense of identity, my self-absorption, scatters with the leaves. For most of us our closest companion is *us*. To each of us it is we who are most real to ourselves. It is almost inconceivable that we would willingly lose this companion with whom, through whom, we think we experience the world. That is how it is for me too, usually. Long ago, however, as a small boy, I had intimations that there was something more behind who I thought I was. I had no words for it. No one I knew had any words for it—this profound sense there was no one home. Not emptiness exactly, but not individuality either. My experience of it was deep but erratic. Most of the time I did not experience its immediacy, and these were very lonely times because I found I could talk to no one about it. What would a child know about such things?

In one way or another I have spent my life trying to understand this *no one* within. This book is in part about that struggle. Somewhere in my early adulthood, well before I came to Zen practice, I tagged it with the name *St. Nadie* (nah-dee-ay), a Spanish word meaning *no one*. Looking back, I am sure I used *Saint* as an unconscious comment on the Saints of my Irish Catholic childhood—beings of unattainable sanctity, watching over us all the time. It has stuck in my consciousness, sacred and secret, a kind of non-guardian angel. St. Nadie. No one. No one goes this Way . . . though always present, usually hidden, older and more real than myself.

And this reality *I* experience? We think we can escape *into* reality from dream and fantasy, that there, wherever that is, is where we will find surety, harmony, sense, knowledge that this is true. It has been suggested that this utopian need to piece together the fragments of experience into a restored whole is the central strand of Western thought. As science has come to subsume philosophical thought, we assume we know the right questions and that for each there is an answer that is correct. How easy it is to ignore that we are ourselves at the center of this asking, and that all means for asking and answering come from us. We pretend the truth of something is true in spite of us, but we are only interested in knowable things, including the truth. The arrogance of this position, that unknowable answers are not genuine, has always seemed sad and peculiar to me, and a bit incoherent.

A friend of mine, a scientist and logician by trade, reminded me that science is a method of knowledge by description and that, on the whole, scientists think that the terms, the language we use to ask questions and formulate answers, that the terms and mathematics of science *mean* this or that. "They don't," he said, "They never did. . . . There is the math. There is the world. And there is the structural correspondence. That's it." He recognizes this is a conditional way of knowing and a limited one. He says that terms of math and logic are inadequate to communicate literal experience, or what he calls knowledge by acquaintance (after, I suppose, Bertrand Russell). He suggests poetry and art are all we have to communicate what we know by experience.

So at best we have descriptive models of bits and pieces dependent upon our ability to identify exactly—a conditional perspective. I believe there is a sneaking suspicion among us that, handy as these models are, they are not enough. The language of poetry, the act of poetry, is maddening and wonderful—uncertain. There is a plurality of possibility— and impossibility. For me, poetry has become the voice of my inner no one, of St. Nadie. Recognizing the differences in the ways of knowing is not to give one ascendancy over another but to recognize that understanding the reality of human experience is not satisfied by either or both. There is no one thread, no complex whole, no real answer in the way we want the *real* to be.

Our history of dissatisfaction is getting pretty long. The duality inherent in these ways of knowing continues to feed our persistence. We demand defining judgment to affirm ourselves, but it has never been forthcoming into the conditional way we experience. At the same time we know in a literal way that we are not visitors. It is the paradox of being and the burden of mortality. This is it. We are afraid.

> Unknown answers
> scatter empty roads,
> brittle leaf music.

Part I

THE DEATH OF THE FATHERS

1

END OF THE RATIONAL IDEAL

What makes a life? What makes its choices? Who am I when I stand before another? Before myself in a mirror—and the many things *are* all mirrors? Who is this when I am alone and nameless, sitting in the woods with sleeping trees and snowy dusk? The answers are always conditional.

Is it where you live? I have an American passport. But I was born in Munich of an Irish mother and an Irish-American father who was then a soldier stationed there after the war. I have a German birth certificate. Does this make me German or American? I know what I have a right to claim, but that does not answer the question. I can claim citizenship through my grandparents. My paternal grandfather was from Belfast. Does that make me Irish or English? It depends upon whom you ask. My grandmother, his wife, was Czech. Her country does not even exist now as it did for her. What does that say about me? Nothing.

I have lived for thirty years in Upstate New York. This is not Westchester County or the Hudson Valley, but the real Upstate that has its own weather section in the *Farmer's Almanac*. Up here that thirty years makes me merely a "longtime resident." My wife is a "native," born here as her mother was. But I have also lived and worked or studied in Liberia, the Canary Islands, England, and Puerto Rico. I used to consider my roots to be in the rural Delaware Valley, where I was a small child. Now, I don't know.

Perhaps it is what you do? I used to hate that question. In America the common way of finding out *who* a person is comes from posing a question about *what* they *do*. "Hi, I'm Bob. I'm an engineer. What do you do?" It saves a lot of probing guesswork. One is either this or that and whatever our stereotypes about that happen to be, we find ourselves satisfied by them. And it is true that many people identify themselves with their work. Can you think of any medical doctor who would not say he or she was a doctor when asked who they were? I could say, for example, that my dad was a grocer, for he worked in grocery stores, supermarkets, and the food business most of his adult life. But that hardly explains the complex and troubled man who gave me a copy of Voltaire when I was only fifteen.

When our children were small, I stayed at home as the primary caregiver. This was unusual at the time. My wife's career in industry was just beginning to blossom. I had by then been a teacher at a small prep school in Pennsylvania, a lecturer in American literature at a Spanish University, a freelance writer with one book to my name (from a small press that immediately after went out of business), and had sold the independent bookstore I had owned and operated for seven years. I worked at night teaching business communications and American literature at the adult education extension of the local community college. I wrote poems while the children napped and I created paintings on weekends.

I learned quickly not to say I was a homemaker. People would wince as they tried to place a Betty Crocker template over me and my firm handshake. Nor would I say I was a poet or an artist. Despite national poetic figures as wildly different as Robert Frost and Allen Ginsberg, the stereotype of the Oscar Wilde aesthete tiptoeing through the tulips was what came to mind for many of the people I would meet. I'd say I was a writer and taught at MVCC. That was okay. It had a ring to it. But it wasn't who I was.

Even after fourteen years working in rare books and manuscripts at a research library, with a master's in library science and professional publications, I do not call myself a librarian. After doing consulting work for UNESCO in Germany I find I could also call myself a documentalist, but I don't. For six years I've worn the shaved head of an ordained Rinzai Zen monk, but unless people ask me about my head (and some do!) I rarely mention it, despite my deep involvement as a clergyman in our community. It is because of who I am that I am a monk, not the other way around.

Perhaps it is the way you live or what has happened to you? Are you handicapped? A widow? A Catholic? A Jew? A victim (of what)? And me? I'm a drunk, an alcoholic. Twelve years ago I went into rehab and have been working at recovery ever since. For six of those years I taught meditation to other alcoholics and addicts at a local rehabilitation unit. My twelfth-step work. When I finally went for help, I was a tenth of an inch from losing everything—job, family, life. I have absolutely no doubt that if I had continued as I was I'd be dead now. This is the real thing. I am not afraid to talk about it but neither do I advertise it. I was told that if I wanted to get better I had to completely change my life. Yeah, right, I thought. I was forty-one. I was me. I could be a good boy and not drink any more, but I could not change who I was. I was wrong. I am not the same person I was twelve years ago. I could not have predicted who I became, nor how substantively different. Clearly, being an alcoholic is not a defining characteristic.

Vanity is such a subtle thing. Twice a year I am supposed to attend intensive "retreats" called *sesshin* at a traditionally run Buddhist monastery in the mountains, as part of my training as a monk. It is the kind of training one comes to realize has no end point. It is a lifelong way of keeping in shape spiritually. One of the two sesshin is always supposed to be Rohatsu Sesshin. This is an eight-day affair that takes place in the first week in December, ending on December 8, the day that traditionally marks the Buddha's awakening. It is the most demanding and the most rewarding sesshin, with up to fourteen hours of meditation a day. The mountains can be beautiful in December. One year a heavy snowfall wiped out power in a three county area and temperatures in the *zendo* (the meditation hall) dropped to thirty-three degrees. But we just put on long-johns under our robes and sat in a silence so deep (no heat pipes, no white noise, no water running, no lights humming) we could hear the snowflakes settle outside. We were transported back three hundred years to a monastic experience impossible almost anywhere today.

In December of 1997, I was sitting through my eighth Rohatsu and my fifteenth or sixteenth sesshin at the monastery. Compared to some participants, I was still in my sesshin adolescence, but I was not a newcomer. I knew from experience that the first two or three days are the most difficult, rather like on a wilderness canoe trip, then one toughens up and truly enters into the rhythms of the extraordinary silent dance sesshin becomes. But this time I did not toughen up. Pain in my legs and back increased each day. The little sleep we got was erratic at best for me. By the sixth day I was nearly passing out from pain. But I refused to say anything to anyone. We do learn how to deal with pain, and I was convinced I was failing to do so in some way, weakening in my resolve. Certainly Rohatsu in a Rinzai monastery breeds a kind of samurai attitude, a sense of toughness—we are the Dharma Marines! This may be helpful in some circumstances, though I am not so sure what they might be. It nearly killed me, at any rate. I would not let myself see something was indeed wrong with me—not a failure of will (ironic in this ego-eradicating environment) but of my body. I would not listen to the warning signals. I was very sick.

It took some time for the doctors to get it right because the symptoms are easily disguised as something else. Besides, men who grew up as athletes, as I did, tend to hold on to the notion they are immortal and don't need doctors anyway, so I didn't even mention at first some of the things bugging me. I thought they'd go away by themselves. But I was finally diagnosed with Graves' Disease, a hyperthyroid condition rare in men. The pain I experienced at Rohatsu came from loss of muscle tone in my body as my overactive thyroid consumed my proteins. I was so convinced I was beyond egotistic concerns for myself I couldn't see my arrogance of denial. Subtle indeed. Does this make me an invalid (curious word in this context, if you shift the accent a little . . .)? No, I am getting better. It's serious, permanent, but manageable, like a low-grade diabetes. This humbling lesson has not, however, changed who I am. Something else has and I am still discovering what that something is.

The American Soto Zen teacher Dennis Genpo Merzel writes in *The Eye Never Sleeps*: "We think life and death [or sickness and health] are separate phenomena. We never think of life and death as the same, that would be illogical. Only one problem . . . reality is not logical. Truth is not rational; only our minds are. We are so egotistical, so arrogant, that we want to make reality into a concept, reduce life to a logical idea. We spend all our time looking for some concept of Truth, but Truth is what is left when we drop all concepts." Who is not dying or ill in some way? Death is the one thing at which we cannot fail.

Vimalakirti says: "All sentient beings are ill, therefore I am ill. My sickness will last as long as there is ignorance and self-clinging. As long as beings are sick, I myself will remain sick."

It is a way of saying I will remain human. Merzel comments on this: "When we are trying to be strong, defending ourselves, we can't let ourselves get sick. We force ourselves to stay well because we don't feel strong enough to be vulnerable. . . . Delusion is a concept; enlightenment is a concept. Health is a concept; sick is another concept. We seek after health and try to avoid sickness, seek after enlightenment and try to avoid delusion. All are just concepts! Without concepts we find ourselves unbounded, undefined; and our greatest fear is to live without boundaries, without definitions. . . Everyone and everything can come in." When my own health broke, something hard and bitter in me broke as well. There stood No One.

This is how we begin—in the morning with small birds near and echoing train yards in the distance—afraid. Exactly like one another. If the grass, the trees, the small birds, the snow, the wind, and all things living and inanimate belong each to themselves, to whom do we belong? I am you when you are alone and nameless, before any river or tree, when the darkness before the stars itself was fearless.

A Sweetness Appears and Prevails

The reason we bother
to get up in the morning
is because of everything;
is because there is another arithmetic
without internal sense
and we ache at the borders;
is because the grey music
of the first chickadee before dawn
in the hemlocks
is the grinding engines of the humpyard
carried on morning air;
is because we are afraid
and know everyone is afraid
and do not know
who will soothe our tears
nor how many tears
we will hold unshed.
You seem to be you
and I seem to be me.
My sorrows are no greater
than your sorrows.
Thou art beautiful,
o my loves,
as tears are.

In a universe of so-called oneness what is not the same? We want it to be us. And we do not want it. The Chilean poet Cecelia Vicuños writes: "In Nahuatl, one of the names for God is 'nearness and togetherness.'" We wish to be unique and together at once. It is a kind of sadness, this longing.

There is a mathematician and glass artist I know who claims we are simply our bodies and that our bodies are our memories, not the magnetic tape computer model, but an inchoate mass of all we have experienced from which we select our particular past to be who we think we are. It is the latter part of this equation that is mutable. Borges pushes this vision to the limit in his small story "Funes the Memorious," in which a boy comes to remember absolutely everything without any choosing and becomes incapable of thinking about *who* or *what* at all. "To think is to forget differences, generalize, make abstractions. In the teaming world of Funes, there were only details, almost immediate in their presence. . . . Funes could continuously discern the tranquil advances of corruption, of decay, of fatigue. He could note the progress of death, of dampness. He was the solitary and lucid spectator of a multiform, instantaneous and almost intolerably precise world." We are not our memories. We are not spectators. "Think about what you are saying. Do not think about what you are saying."

There is a word that comes to us from the Middle Low German that means to be tongue-tied. Not so much that one cannot think what to say but that the experience is so beyond words and the conditions defined by words and their reasoned order that the tongue is tied by expressing silence. It is *mumchance*. It is the experience one has confronting something beyond meaning. When something "means" it means for *us*. I am tongue-tied when I confront what *is*, as it is, with no *me* as a referent. It is accepting a sense that is not our understanding.

This situation has something to do with a new experience of faith—not faith as we all learned it: a compulsory belief in something we can't really know. That was faith as an ideal. This is more of what a friend of mine in AA calls "a willingness to take the next step even though you don't know what will happen." It is seeing the "truth" of every stone, every tree, every wind without concepts of truth or words to define it. The late Iris Murdoch suggests that this concerned attention "effects a removal from the usual egotistic fuzz of self-protective anxiety. One may not be sure that those who observe stones and snails lovingly will also thus observe human beings, but such observation is a *way*, an act of respect for individuals, which is itself a virtue, and an image of virtue." When I become without boundaries, I know without fear I am no one.

Mumchance

It is not for understanding
nor clarity of meaning
I listen carefully to you,
late thrush
across the meadows.

2

THE END OF PERFECTION

The spiritual life is often described as being on a path. It implies direction, purpose, and an end. Even an endless path suggests to us an evolution toward some kind of perfection. One is either on it or off it. I think I can tell those who are on it from those who are not. I am not—or if I am, I am on it only tentatively, by default, an accident, or some mistake. Some day I'll be found out and bumped off by those who deserve to be on it. I can never reach perfection, though I assume it's out there.

Buddhists sometimes refer to the wayless way or the pathless path. To enter the way of the Dharma is to enter a territory without maps. Maps and paths are concepts. Concepts no longer apply. This is terrifying to most of us (especially if we are trying to find our *selves!*). The Lotus Sutra says the Buddha's teachings are like the wind, powerful but without a discoverable source, leaving no trace in the sky.

There is a wonderful scene in the film *"Black Robe,"* a film about the coming of Jesuitical Christianity to Canada in the early seventeenth century. A group of men are traveling by canoe. They are a mix of trappers, Jesuit priests, and Native American guides, the latter tentatively converted to Christianity. The canoes come around a bend. The spreading vista of a lake and deeply forested eastern mountains opens before them. It is a breathtaking scene of wilderness at the edge of winter, just before the first snows, before the grey waters freeze.

Totally still, silent, vast, sleeping. One of the priests gasps. He curses the landscape as a God-forsaken, demon-ridden realm, wild, outside God's laws. He is afraid. To him it is like death. It is without guarantees. It is without maps, wildly imperfect, without order, directionless, chaos. There is no reasoning with it.

Later in the film, the lead guide is wounded in a skirmish with a band of hunting Iroquois. The wound is mortal and he asks to be left to die on an island in the lake. The Jesuits struggle with this but eventually give in to his wishes, for he has become a burden to their mission. They pray for him and ask him to believe and that then God would admit him to heaven. But he does not believe. He has dreamed of this place and now realizes the dreams were death dreams. As his daughter paddles away with the Black Robes, she sees his spirit rise out of his body. He is smiling the smile of soul peace as his spirit walks toward the trees, his hand in the hand of the She-Manitou, the messenger of the Creator, to "walk the ghost trail in the stars." It was not for him a question of belief or hope. It just was as it is. If you are the answer you cannot know the answer, you can only be the answer. Being cannot be acquired. We desire acquired wisdom (science) to become infused wisdom (Dharma). That isn't how it works.

Until recently, I thought I first met St. Nadie in a not-very-coherent poem I wrote about twenty years ago, called "St. Nadie in Winter." I did not recognize the voice had always been with me. It is clear to me now I was only half listening to the voice all that time. The poem had some surprising bits in it that I did not understand but that I knew held the seeds of something interesting.

I spent many lines trying to make what I sensed to be important to come out. But I was in the middle of my long, painful apprenticeship to the art of poetry and, like any apprentice, I did not have the master's perspective. Desire, death, remembering, freedom, and fear were things I had not lived sufficiently. I was so busy looking for meaning for *me* I couldn't hear the wisdom of No One. I ended up playing a game of words and pretend. We do not leave make-believe behind when we emerge into so-called adulthood. We just call it rationalization. It is said rationalization is more important to life than money, food, or sex. While we can get through weeks, months, even years without some of these others, it is impossible to get through a single day without rationalizing something. How difficult it is to know the actuality of our inner voice, to know it is not some fiction we have created, a rationalized mask over our own godless wildness. I wanted to be free of myself and was at the same time afraid that to be so was a kind of death.

From St. Nadie in Winter

With a lamp and keys
Desire prowls among these trees
crippled with diseased soil.
Do not meet it.
It will eat any scrawny wish,
swallow you whole.
. . . .

Is it only the Dead say something
worth remembering,
or is it each small soul bent,
huddled outside the enemy camp,
genius and immortality grey or broken
in its hands?
. . . .

A crow flaps and is still
in the dead harpy's worms.
. . . .

Who does not wish to be air
free of itself
alone in red sky?

Life continuously refuses to show us the plot. The desire to give life shape, and by shape, meaning, is so great anything will do. But Orwell would have us stand against all the "smelly little orthodoxies which are now contending for our souls." I am struck by how difficult it is to get back to something we knew to be true once we have been converted, forced by circumstances, or simply denied and turned away from that knowledge, to whatever lonely mess we have managed to make since. It is as though the experience of unhappiness were more valid than that of joy. We all know the experience of wanting something badly, only to have it disappear as we approach it. Rarely do we look at the wanting self. My shadowless shadow. We don't cope with much grace, neither the grace of civility, nor the grace of physical being, nor the grace of the spirit. There is at bottom no real distinction between them anyway. Perhaps I am too often absent from my own being.

When I was eighteen or nineteen I lived with my parents and sisters on Tenerife, the largest of the Canary Islands. At the northeast tip of the island is a mountain pine forest called Las Mercedes. We lived a short ride from there, near the old city of La Laguna. One day I determined to take a camping trip to the forest. I borrowed a sleeping bag from a colleague of my father's; a strange and testy Dane named Steen, who hated to lose at chess, though he usually did, even against inept me. I took a skin of wine, a loaf of the crusty local bread, some cheese, and fruit in a pack with the sleeping bag and made my way by bus. I don't recall what I said to my father or sisters, but I told my mother I was going for a *mystical* experience. Odd as it may seem, she accepted this. She knew I had an intense relationship with nature. She used to joke with friends, when I was little, "Terry is so cute. He talks to trees." I had been feeling myself slipping away from that "conversation."

I took the bus one afternoon to the end of the long valley, east out of La Laguna. There was a small grotto by the bus stop used for picnics and as a toilet by those awaiting the bus. I found a trail leading up the mountains and followed it. The day was sunny and dry, the scent of pine heady in the air. I crossed a road and continued upward, following a trail leading into the mountains that kept disappearing and then reappearing in odd places. I began to pause frequently, partly from the steady climb, partly from the slippery footing of the pine needles on the forest floor. There was little undergrowth. Just before dusk I reached a ridge. The trees grew right to the top of it. I found a small bowl-like indentation in the slope about ten feet across, filled with pine needles, that faced southwest. I decided to settle there for the night, hoping for my "experience" while the sun set, as though I could schedule an insight into the true nature of the universe. I took out my food and ate half of everything, happily watching the sun go down. It was lovely, but nothing "happened." I crawled up to the ridge, overcoming my fear of heights somehow, and looked over. It dropped off suddenly several thousand feet, but instead of darkening forest and ocean, I saw a sea of grey as a vast bank of clouds spread just below me. With the cooling air after sunset, the clouds began to rise toward me and flow over the top, filling my side of the forest with thick fog and a soft, misty rain that was part of the air itself. It became cold and damp. I pulled my clothes and food into the sleeping bag and hunkered down for a long, silent, wet night. I was tired from the long climb, so I slept regardless.

The first edges of grey light and the dawn birds woke me. I sat up stiff and wet. Cold. Feeling a bit sorry for myself. Disappointed I didn't have the special moment I had come for. I took a leak, watching the little yellow river flow under the pine needles and down the slope. My bread and cheese had remained dry, so I made a small breakfast for myself and washed it down with the remaining wine in the skin. Then I just sat there for a while. I stopped assessing the situation and joined the still trees as the last of the fog drifted down toward the valley. No sound but the soundless sound of fog moving off in the sunrise. After some time, I have no idea of how much, there was a kind of music off to my left. Someone was whistling a tune. I heard footsteps and saw a young man, perhaps only a few years older than myself, striding down the trail. He burst into song briefly, into one of the local *cantos folkloricos*, and then continued whistling as he forgot the words again, on down the mountain. He never saw me among the pines. I remained still as the whistling faded. Some resistance in me followed the whistling away and I was suddenly filled with a great and inexplicable love for this stranger singing in the morning. For the silent trees around me. The welling love burst me, or rather there was in that instant no me to burst, only the forest, the mountain, the teeming, sun-misted valley all humming and huge and breathing itself.

Times later (seconds, hours, eons) I found myself again, shaking, tears running freely down my face. Whence this vast exhausting unconditional love? I used to marvel at the story of St. Tarcisius, whose name seemed a little like mine, who was martyred holding the Host against his breast. I felt this burning joy in my own breast as I methodically and neatly gathered my things and walked home, the whole way, ignoring the bus, past farms and dogs and the outlying hamlets. By the time I got home, dusty and quiet, I had banked the coals of that fire into a corner of my inner hearth.

This was not an occasion for exalted self-feeling. It was not forced, though initially I had tried to force it. It was not reasoned attention to nature or to myself but an experience to which I could avail myself only by dropping any pretense of a participating individuality or self. And I had to drop it without thinking about dropping it. The completion, the presence, brooked no inner nor outer sensibility, no being part of nor being apart from. I never spoke of the experience. I never questioned its reality, but, as I had with similar ones when I was younger, I learned not to say much about them. Imagine my shock of recognition when I discovered these lines in Wordsworth's *Prelude*:

> Oft in these moments such a holy calm
> Would overspread my soul, that bodily eyes
> Were utterly forgotten, and what I saw
> Appeared like something in myself. . . .

I was not alone. No one is alone. This is the first understanding.

A professor of religion I know at Syracuse University once declared that the "Age of Miracles" is past, that insight experiences are no longer possible in our empirical world. He is wrong. It was through such experiences, affirmed by reading in Wordsworth, and through these words I read at sixteen in Joyce's *Portrait of the Artist as a Young Man*, that I decided to give up dreams of being a botanist or some sort of scientist, according to family wishes and my own desire to be with plants, to become a writer: "Welcome, O Life! I go to encounter for the millionth time the reality of experience and to forge in the smithy of my soul the uncreated consciousness of my race."

There is something I chant every morning. The words are in Pali and said to be the words that Shakyamuni spoke on his deathbed, his final and greatest message:

> *Attadīpā*
> *Viharatha*
> *Attasaraṇā*
> *Anaññasaraṇā*
>
> *Dhammadīpā*
> *Dhammasaraṇā*
> *Anaññasaraṇā*

The translation I like best is:

> You are the Light itself!
> Do not be afraid.
> You are the refuge of the Light.
> There is no other refuge.
>
> You are the truth itself.
> Light of the Truth!
> Refuge of the Truth!

When I told my teacher I wished to be ordained, she said, "Who is this who wants to be a monk?" I sat with that for many days. One early morning the Sangha was chanting "Attadīpā." It has a lovely sing-song quality that most of our chanting, in the Japanese style, does not. As we settled into *zazen* (seated meditation) after the chanting, I let the modest tunefulness trail around in my brain for a little, saying the syllables over and over. At some point the meaning of the words slipped into the flow: you are the Light itself! Suddenly I was flooded with light and tears, not unlike the morning on the mountain, and I knew the answer to the question, not just in my head but in my blood and bones: Attadīpā, the Light itself. There is no wishing. There is no monk. There is the Light itself, as Soen Roshi loved to say, already and always.

The metaphor of the bird, which comes and goes without leaving a trace in the air, whose song goes no-one-knows-where after it is heard, is commonly used for the wayless way. I turn, further, to alcoholics and addicts, those who have reached their bitter bottom where choice has been removed by addiction, where learned values and sense are overruled by a sickness that can allow one to rationalize behavior that will kill (alcoholism is usually fatal and can only be arrested). Such people are my companions, not just reminders of what it is like to have choices removed, to be a prisoner of a socially stigmatized disease, but because I am one of them. Then how do we mean?

Picture a small boy looking out his bedroom window at dawn. He sees below him a walled-in garden under very old trees, the brick walls heavy with ivy. There is the scent of green on the air, of apples, of earth and manure from the nearby farm. The grass in the garden is wet and the small flowers are heavy with dew. In the garden he watches a woman with long white hair, the first time he has seen it long, let down. She is walking barefoot. Her nightgown and robe are wet at the bottom. She is holding a cup of tea, walking very slowly, talking to her plants softly, words he cannot quite hear, until he realizes they are words she has never spoken to anyone, they are Czech, her birth tongue. He senses, without words of his own to articulate it, that this is a private moment, how she places herself into her day. The unexpected intimacy moves him deeply. Though he witnesses it again over the years, this first touch of an inner other stays with him—what it is to be with another without judgment, to enter their vulnerability, a sudden unsought intimacy that eliminates "other." It is the intimation that the "light itself" has no boundaries.

I Am Not Ready to Be Without

Once upon a time
once and for all went away
without a trace.
The drunk—his heart bewildered,
he has become my companion.
The flying bird—
pathless in the winter sky,
she has become my heart.

3

THE END OF LINEAR CERTAINTIES

To have something to say is to be a person. But speaking
depends on listening and being heard; it is
an intensely relational act.
—CAROL GILLIGAN CITED BY KATE O'NEILL
IN *Buddhist Women on the Edge*

Each day at work I encounter what Isaiah Berlin calls, with only a
little melodrama, "the inflamed desires of the insufficiently regarded to
count for something among the cultures of the world"—in this case the
culture of working in an academic research library. There are two hundred employees here. Our work is largely service. Each of us would like
our work to count for something, for ourselves to count for something.
Usually we do not experience either. There are many people who are
lonely and afraid. We recently survived a strike by unionized support
staff with all the attendant acrimony. Yet the administrators are not bad
people. They are really quite ordinary. It often seems to me a case of
loneliness in Herder's sense: "To be lonely is to be among people who
do not know what you mean." However mindfully we witness our own
experience, if it does not include that of others, we remain lost in it.
A shade is not the whole darkness. But the arrogance of our Western
linearity, where we hold to the singularity of our own experience of the

world, denies a deeper relativity we all sense, that gives the lie to any single moral and intellectual universe.

Buddhism does not interpret, does not place values, which are necessarily conditional. To say the end of truth or morality is the beginning of nihilism is just another duality, a mere pairing of concepts. It is a way of copping out—saying "Nothing matters, I'm not responsible."

A person has every right to say, "So what? How about me? I'm more than this. I'm less than this. You don't know what I am or mean." But we all have something to say and a need to be heard, a responsibility to listen. To listen, to hear with an open heart, we have to know forgiveness, perhaps Christianity's greatest single gift to the world, as well as its most ignored. In a prayer we recite regularly, the Bodhisattva's Vow, we are admonished to be warm and compassionate toward those who would turn against us. Even if they abuse and persecute us we should see them as teachers. But the real test comes when you change the pronoun from *them* to *us*. "Even though *we* may be fools . . . if by chance *we* should turn against *ourselves* . . . by *our own* egoistic delusion and attachment." If you can forgive yourself, "who can be ungrateful or not respectful, even to senseless things, not to speak of a man or a woman"—or ourselves. Here we find the beginnings of understanding what it means when there is no one to forgive . . . when first we forgive ourselves.

In *The Death of Ivan Ilyich*, Tolstoy writes, "What if my entire life, my entire conscious life, was not the real thing?" I've been asked that if this were true of me, if the answer were yes, could I forgive myself? For what? Living a lie? I have had to, and coming to the place where I could face the lie has been a long journey. We are not asking for something wiser, better, or more perfect but for something authentically real for us as human beings, real as we are real, imperfect, incomplete. This humble and humbling attitude has the effect of allowing us to revere what is.

During the winter we sit down to breakfast half an hour before sunrise. Through the window by the table, in the grey light under the cedars, I watch juncos land on the birdfeeder's metal roof and slide down the new powdery snow to the feeding bar. At first they seem startled, but then they do it again and again. Small winter birds sledding at breakfast. May we find each other in this experience.

In a direct, linear way we see desperation approaching, wordless, enveloping, inevitable. But it is not inevitable. We have a choice how to respond (unless we have given over our choice to addiction). The wisdom by which we are able to realize in ourselves the truth of a thing must not be only intellectual. It needs an element of attentive affection. One of the names for the Buddha—any Buddha—is Tathagata. It is usually translated as "thus come." It also, at the same time, means "thus gone. It makes no difference. At the turn of this paradox, just as we suspect that birth was the death of us, in the midst of total uncertainty, we can love.

Loathe to Leave You to Your Death

When you are no good,
when you are fodder,
when your ground is soiled,
when the precious child leaves you
without looking back,
when your truth is falsified
by terror and death,
when all doors are ashes
and all walls are deaf,
when your breath tastes like iron,
when you will never know a day
without some sort of aching,
you are beautiful
o my loves
as tears are,
comely as the first holy snow.

Part II

THE ORPHANED DARK

4

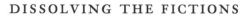

DISSOLVING THE FICTIONS

On a Thursday evening in late spring you can hear children at play in the street through the open window. And birds yattering away, clamoring for territory, for mates, for the pure joy of it, who knows. The zendo is silent. Sixteen or seventeen people sit in two rows, one of which bends around the "ell" in the attic room. This is the old zendo of our early days on the third floor of our spiritual director's home, a century-old Victorian pile.

Many of those sitting in the silent room first came to the zendo as I did. I was in crisis. I was scared. For the first time I could actually see the bottom of the barrel and it was the abyss. My drinking had taken control of my life. No single moment went by without planning for it in relation to drinking. My marriage was tearing badly at the seams. I had found I could not write without drinking to give me that creative buzz, but by this time, I had to drink so much just to get the buzz I couldn't hold a pen. My job was just a matter of time. The inner life, my spiritual being where my writing lived, was dying almost as assuredly as my body was. For seventeen years I had practiced Transcendental Meditation with fair regularity but without a guide. I had been on a plateau for years and had now come to the cliff at its end. I gave up meditation. This was not for me a small thing. It was connection. I was not sure to what, but it was real. Now it was gone.

Most people who knew me then assumed my first real step toward recovery was when I agreed to go to counseling, but that was more than a year after I first made an appointment at the Zen Center of Syracuse. I knew I needed help and I thought I knew where to begin. I suppose I also thought, quite wrongly as it turns out, that if I got my spiritual act together, the drinking and all of the other problems would take care of themselves.

I was in the local New-Age bookstore and saw a poster for the Zen Center. I asked the manager about it and was told it was "the real thing," not just a hang-out for aging hippies (as his store was). I called the number. The soft woman's voice on the phone assured me she was the director. She asked me some questions in a hesitant tone and we made an appointment. I later understood her hesitation. Many odd people would call the Zen Center and she needed to make sure their interest in Zen was real. The Zen Center was in her home.

I arrived at the appointed time, standing nervously on the front porch, noticing the toys there. Young children lived here too. A small, pleasant-looking woman, with cropped grey hair, answered the door. She asked me to remove my shoes, something that has since become a habit in my own home, and took me up a back staircase off the kitchen and through a bathroom, to the attic. The house was a happy clutter of books (piles and groaning cases), art (every available surface had a picture), artifacts, toys. Off the attic landing was a door. She opened it to a long room, radical in its uncluttered purity. The zendo. We sat facing one another and I have no recollection of what we discussed. I was overwhelmed with a sense of homecoming. I knew I had found my teacher, someone who, should I ever be able to have some sort of insight, would be able to see and affirm that I did.

By the time of this pleasant spring evening I had been through rehab and had been sitting for a few years. It was evening but there was still light enough to see by. We all enjoyed the natural waning light of day. The room was, as I say, silent. There were a few more women than men. Folk's ages varied: a few students, a few adults with families, adults going back to school, adults with jobs of various kinds, a professor, a researcher, a macramé artist, a painter or writer, a couple of individuals from industry—the usual mix in a lay practice near a university.

Whatever each individual's inner struggle, there was a palpable sense of enjoyment in the room. After a long day of work it is good to sit with these good people, share silence and peace. Each of them had once felt that sense of coming home I experienced on my first visit. It is renewed as we sit together in the gloaming.

Mothers begin to call the children in. The birds' roosting songs draw to a close. A dog barks in another neighborhood. Darkness deepens in the room. You can touch the stillness. Out of nowhere her voice booms: "Are you waiting for your life to happen? Or are you tasting it *now*?"

In the Beckett play *Endgame* Clove asks Hamm, "Do you believe in the life to come?" Hamm replies, "Mine was always that."

I once loved a woman who was always angry with me. She said I lived my life vicariously, trying to fulfill someone else's expectations of what my life *should* be, that I was waiting to finally get it right for everyone, then I could live my own life. She said she wasn't going to wait for the real me forever. She didn't stick around and I didn't learn, though as I look back perhaps what she wanted was her version of me. Recently I discovered when some of the seeds of this apparent attitude of mine were planted. I never went to kindergarten. When I started school in first grade parochial schools were crowded, often fifty students to a class. Maybe I wasn't ready. I found most of the work easy and boring. I would spend the entire day staring out the window. Sometimes, of course, I was wishing I was outside (I threw myself absolutely into recesses and always came home dusty and grass-stained). But mostly I was dreaming, making up stories, my mind afire. I had to stay nearly every day after school because I had not completed the work with the other kids. Usually I could get through the incomplete work quickly, especially when the terrifying second grade nun, Sister Sarah, was watching, her grey face peering through the glass of the classroom door. But I began to learn that people had expectations and that in order to get them off my case I had to start pretending to fulfill their expectations. I never thought that the expectations might have any value for me. They were their expectations, after all. By the time I was ten I had forgotten why I was pretending and so living other's wishes became real.

Many of us have such stories where someplace between then and now we have gotten lost. The way back is easier than we could have imagined. It is right here in whatever we do each day. The "practice" at the Zen Center of Syracuse (ZCS) is a lay practice. It is founded on the simple understanding that if Buddhist practice cannot help ordinary people live ordinary lives more completely, then it is not much good for anything. One should not have to become a special case or live in extraordinary circumstances in order to grasp the fundamentals. Zen emphasizes ordinary day-to-day things because when we grasp the essential emptiness in the least thing we simultaneously apprehend it in the universe.

The novelist Masao Abe has said, "In our daily life, there are moments when we are *here* with ourselves—moments in which we feel a vague sense of unity. But at other moments we find ourselves *there*—looking at ourselves from the outside. We fluctuate between here and there from moment to moment: homeless, without a place to settle." He goes on to add that only humans experience this divisive self-consciousness, that plants and other animals just are what they are.

On the positive side, while we live self-consciously, we think, create human culture, science, and art—we think about how to live and how to develop our lives. But we do it looking from the outside and are thus separated from ourselves. Abe says, "So far as we are moving between here and there, between inside and outside, looking at ourselves in comparison with others, and looking at ourselves from the outside, we are always restless. . . . Insofar as one is a human being, one cannot escape this basic anxiety."

In a talk on Sufism, Thomas Merton, in an aside, cites Martin Buber: "In Eden Adam and Eve could do only good. It was their nature to do good. They could not be or do otherwise. There was not in their frame of reference anything other than good, so there was no real good in the sense that it is something opposing evil. Evil was not in the picture. What they came to desire through Satan's temptation was to see themselves doing good."

Abe goes on similarly about this theme, "God created a tree as a tree and saw that it was good: it is in *suchness* as a tree. . . . Everything is in its own *suchness*. It was the same when he created Adam and Eve. . . . They are just as they are." But, as we know, according to Genesis, Adam and Eve ate the fruit of the knowledge of good *and* evil. This is more than a question of ethics. Abe suggests, "The eating of the fruit suggests the making of value judgments. . . . The ability to make value judgments is a quality unique to self-consciousness. . . . By means of self-consciousness we also make a distinction between ourselves and others. As a consequence of this distinction, we become attached to self, making ourselves the center of the world." This is the sin of Eden. And it is ours.

Buddhism regards self-consciousness as ignorance, a loss of awareness of the reality of our suchness. Our outside view of ourselves is a basic ignorance inherent in human existence. Masao Abe continues, "As long as the human self tries to take hold of itself through self-consciousness (out of which feelings of inferiority, superiority, etc., develop), the human ego-self falls into an ever-deepening dilemma. At the extreme point of this dilemma, the ego can no longer support itself and must collapse into emptiness. . . . The realization of no-self is a necessity for the human ego. . . . We must realize that there is no unchanging, eternal ego-self."

This is not the end but rather a point of departure. *Suchness* is our ground of being in the world, living without "otherness," without conflict, so each day and each ordinary activity becomes a good day and a good act. This is what is meant by the saying "everything is empty."

He Whose Face Gives No Light Shall Never Become a Star

Deep frost. Sun and moon
at once in the dawn.
Our utter impermanence.
Sudden bitterness
springing all unbidden
at a word
that we will fail again
to be human.

Birds
sleep in the throat.
Behind the ribs
it is a bare open country.
This empty vessel overflowing.

It is odd how the lessons we are given are sometimes not learned for many, many years. When I was about four I was playing one day in my grandfather's studio. It smelled of wood ash, oil paint, and turpentine. It was on the second floor of the two-hundred-year-old house he and my grandmother rented. There was a fireplace, beamed ceilings, dark with age, and bookshelves built in between the corner windows that looked right out over the old coach road. I was moving chess pieces (red and white, oddly enough) around the sloped surface of his desk (the very desk at which I write now), pretending they were soldiers. He shuffled into the room in his slippers, baggy pants, and old cardigan. He stood over me for a few minutes, hand on my shoulder, silently watching me. His hair was still dark and his teeth were brown. He asked if I would sit for him. I knew what this meant. He was working on a portrait of his youngest son, my uncle Brian, then in the Navy. He needed me to sit still with my uncle's Naval cap on my head so he could get the pose and angle right. I agreed because I knew he would talk to me. I loved to hear him talk.

He posed me as he wanted with the cap at a rakish angle over one eye. I thought that it looked stupid and pushed it to the back of my head where I knew it would stay on. He fixed it again. Again I pushed it back. I wore all my cowboy hats like that. He said, "Damn it, keep it like this. Look. Let me tell you a story." And he began, while I became utterly motionless, a story that had been going on for some time. The story featured a glass mountain that was wondrous to see but slippery to climb, a character named Injun Joe of dubious reputation, a number of giants, trolls, and elves, and an absolutely terrifying Big Bad Wolf with yellow eyes, blood dripping from his huge yellow teeth—something that filled my nightmares for many years later.

At some point the story petered out or he became absorbed in some problem on the canvas. Things grew quiet. I could hear the old mahogany grandmother clock, brought over from Ireland and called that because it was smaller than a grand*father* clock, ticking loudly and slowly downstairs.

"Granpop?" I asked suddenly, "Why do you paint?"

He paused, brush in hand, a dark lock over his brow. His eyes, often bleary, became very clear and looked at me as though he had never seen me before. "Well, my son," he said, "Art is a way to talk to God."

Shortly after that, he finished up and freed me to go. I shot down to the kitchen. I had been smelling baking for some time now and had to see what my grandmother was up to. The kitchen was a long, low-ceilinged room that looked out on a dirt road and parking area between the rambly old stone house and the dairy farm next door. As I entered the kitchen I heard the milk pump start up in the barn. My grandmother was leaning over a low table, her hands white with flour. She was making potato rolls, small yeast rolls for which she later became famous. There was a wooden bowl filled with fresh-baked ones. I watched fascinated as she pushed the lively dough with her hands, took an old milk glass dipped in flour, and cut circles with it in the dough. Then she took up each circle, brushed it with butter on half of one side, folded it tenderly and lined it up on a baking sheet. It was all done with economy, speed, and a kind of tenderness I couldn't explain but which was palpable to my young eyes. She did it as intently as my grandfather touched the brush and layered the color on the canvas.

"Gran?" I asked, "Why don't you paint?"

She said, "I'm not an artist."

"But don't you want to talk to God?"

She paused, letting the dough spring back over her fingers as she kneaded. "What do you mean, my little one?"

"Granpop says art is a way to talk to God."

She turned to me, flour up to her elbows, wisps of grey hair about her face, her black eyes boring a hole into me. "My home is my art."

Some mornings I wake up poor. The poverty of longing floods my consciousness with a hollow pain. The dust of regret is a bitter grit on my tongue and stinging the corners of my eyes—even before I am out from under the covers. It is like waking from a dream of standing outside my own house, knocking and knocking, with no one answering.

There is a love that is the affinity of shared harmonies and there is love that is a self-sanctifying gesture, loving one's own image of what another should be. When I am poor such thoughts confuse me. I will lie there wondering what are the reasons I stay in my life? What are the layers of me that come from others, the oughts and shoulds, the visions of others I've accepted and learned to fill. There were times when I wanted someone who needed to be there, to sacrifice on my account as I would on hers, whose eyes looked with mine in the same direction. Even now that such an arrogant and adolescent dream has faded (and I would rather not want at all, or if I must want, would rather at least be with someone wholly in the world), I wake muddled, almost weeping.

My wife of many years lies next to me, rumpled in sleep. I can find myself angered by her vulnerability while longing for intimacy with her. Do I want, for example, sex? It was often deferred, especially in our troubled years just before and into my early recovery, for good and not-so-good reasons, but which were nevertheless seen as normal—to keep peace, to force nothing, to maintain a semblance of harmony. Deferral in sex led to deferral in all important areas so that I began to live vicariously. I settled into inertia and monotony in our relationship as a result of fear. A fear of facing what? That I saw the relationship only in terms of myself? Only partly. Guilt over the grief my drinking brought her and our children? Perhaps. Real intimacy? That meant taking the initiative to share in the evolution of the relationship, even when it did not match the dream we created when we were courting. For many males sex is the only model for intimacy. When intimacy is needed and sex is not possible we turn the perceived failure back in on ourselves, turn it into anger.

It is said anger is self-loathing turned on others. I can believe it. Anger is a power trip, the last resort of the powerless and the assumed right of the powerful. Because it is destructive it seems strong and, so, desirable to the weak. Anger tries to control the present outside of the self. Anger not expressed becomes resentment. Resentment is a way we try to control time, to deny change or its possibility, to deny the feelings of the past have no value in the present. When all wrongs of the past are washed clean, so are all rights! Anger is a cry for "me" to have power outside of the self, refusing to accept *being* as it is, to blame, to fear, to focus all away from the self. Anger destroys—destroys even its source. I used to think some anger was justified. I do not now. Suppose one lets go of power altogether?

But there have been mornings when I awake poor, longing for some physical expression of intimacy, of acceptance of my being in the world. Feeling alone, helpless, unable to express my longing—afraid it will sound like mere selfish desire instead of a need to share our sense of being, I become angry. The feeling comes. Its arrival is not anticipated or thought out or even desired. Long years of habit simply leave the door open for it to enter.

When anger comes upon me I begin to create fictions of the wrongs done to me. I seek out, almost unconsciously, my wife's weak spots when she wakes. I look for the buttons to push. It doesn't take long for her irritated response to the tone of my voice to justify my anger, to define and affirm my loneliness, to push the resentments forward. Eden's sin, to see one's self doing good, turns ugly as I try to see myself justified, right—hating myself for it, denying the hate, pushing on.

One such morning we bickered over the bedclothes. This was when the children were small and I was home during the day. Who was the most restless sleeper? Who mussed the bedding? Over breakfast, would we use the good silver or not for the guests next evening? Can't you even say goodbye without that tone of voice? What tone? And so on. The variations on this theme are as numerous as all the known and unknown Dharma brothers and sisters ever. The cycle must be broken. Who will break it if you do not begin with yourself?

Hanging out laundry in bright beautiful March winds, I muttered to myself, "If only this, if only that." The four letter words I learned from a Danish boatswain, for whom I worked as a deckhand, were getting good exercise. I jammed the clothespins on the line. My fingers were numb. The winds were bright and the temperature below freezing. The cold made me angrier. Early songbirds had returned, but their song was not sweet to me. To me they were squawking over nesting rights. The wind caught a frozen sheet and slapped it in my face. The tape in my head suddenly jammed. There was just the fluttering laundry and the chattering birds. In the empty silence of my brain another song began to emerge, a distant melody just beyond the edge of hearing but not of awareness. What was it? Faint, faint. I reached out for it. It was the lullaby of death, cleansing the loathing, reminding me life is what we have to share.

Lullaby of Death

For though our life may be
a thing to share, who is there
in this world to share our death?
—Brodsky

It's okay.
It's nothing at all.
It does not count.
Nothing has happened.
Everything remains the same.
I am I. You are you
and the old life
is unchanged, untouched.
Whatever we were
we are still.
Call me by the old familiar names.
Speak to me in the easy way
you always used.

5

HABIT OF BEING

I am hopelessly domestic. As much as I love to travel I love being home more. We have a genius for comfortable clutter in our house and I revel in it. I would rather have company than go visit. There is little as satisfying as preparing a meal or sitting by the fire reading to the family, or simply watching the afternoon light stream across the kitchen table transforming ordinary tableware, jars, and bottles into timeless resonant beings and messengers of truth.

Keiji Nishitani speaks of "the importance of sticking closely to every-day life and the problems that arise from that experience, that is, to deal with the problems contained in daily living. . . . The question is: What is the real *face* of our commonplace experience of Daily life?" He goes further, "True reality is encountered while staying in the midst of every day and returning ever more deeply into its depth and inner recesses. Even the great problem of life-and-death is clarified thereby and what is called 'faith' in Buddhism implies a kind of experiencing. Daily life is the basic problem and the last key to all problems. That is the standpoint of Zen and, more generally, the core of the Buddhist standpoint." This is the force, the drive behind the Zen center as a lay practice—what *lay* practice means, to have *naikan*, or thorough-going intuition about ordinary things. The answer is not only in a remote temple but on your kitchen table.

On August 8, 1996, fifty-one years and two days after Hiroshima, a

Buddhist monk was killed by the State of Arkansas. That is one way to tell the story. Another is that Frankie Parker had been on Death Row twelve years and his appeals had finally run out that August day. Both versions are true. In this case the "Dead Man Walking" was one of our *desaparecidos* twice over. He was one of society's throw-aways, an invisible number in our brutal penal system. He was condemned to die. He was also a realized monk, ordained and trained while in prison in a remarkable transformation that was free of self-pity or pride, who could face death with equanimity. Frankie Parker was a confessed murderer, at one time one of the lost who see violence as a real alternative, who could say: "How do you spread the Dharma if the person you meet is blind and dumb? The answer is a hug! Kindness. A hug is a smile, a smile that can be felt. Buddhism is not a religion or philosophy, it is not a psychology or a science. It is example. It is a method of liberation. I feel liberated and soon may be liberated from this world. I change as all things change. . . . I trust that I have not let you down in any way. I trust that this world will be helped in some way by my death. I took refuge in the Buddha. The Dharma and the Sangha gave me refuge. Thank you my friends. Y'all take care . . . live by example!"

For nearly forty years Veronza Bowers has lived in maximum-security prisons. He is a former Black Panther who claims the Feds framed him for murder in the early seventies. He considers himself a political prisoner. It is possible. That is a period needing scrutiny. I do not know the truth of that part of his story and all my wanting to do so cannot change what I cannot know. But I came to know him through my study of the *shakuhachi*, the bamboo flute which is the only melodic instrument used in the Zen tradition. Monty Levenson, who made my flute, also made Veronza's. It was through Monty that I heard about this prisoner who has been denied parole more times than he can count. In prison Veronza turned from someone committed to a violent solution to the racial question into a healer. A man, invisible to us for the better part of a century, who used meditation and music to transform himself. He has studied shiatsu massage, accupressure, and is an honorary elder of the Lompoc California tribe of Five Feathers, a Native American spiritual group. In 1996 he wrote:

> I have lived the past twenty-four years of my life as a Federal prisoner with the Bureau of Prisons number 35316-136 appended to my name. For those of you who have never been inside a maximum-security penitentiary, it might be difficult, if not impossible, to imagine it as a place where the plaintive sounds of shakuhachi can be heard. Ah! But it is true. . . . In the recreation yard of Terre-Haute Federal Penitentiary in Indiana, I first saw Punchy—he being pushed in his wheelchair around the quarter mile track (he had been paralyzed with a gunshot wound); me sitting under the shade of a lone tree blowing my shakuhachi. . . . The song in my heart reflected what I had just seen and my shakuhachi began to cry. . . .

Veronza arranged to work with Punchy to help his healing. After working with him on breathing exercises, accupressure treatments, and stretching, six days a week, two and a half hours a day for a month, they were basically still where they were when they had started. Punchy was locked up inside himself, and Veronza could not reach him. He arranged a meditation session in which he played the flute. During this he achieved a breakthrough of sorts. Punchy is recorded to have said, "It appears that I have allowed the flutist . . . to take me beyond the realms of my control. I can sense serenity, but the pain . . . oh! The pain! And why do I feel as if I'm not alone? . . . My body began to respond, my eyes opened. . . ."

Veronza goes on:

> Ah! The breakthrough! On so many levels a small piece of bamboo, 1.8 feet long, had opened doorways that had previously been shut. Shakuhachi had done in one and a half hours what no human being had done in three years. . . . From

then on we began each working session with shakuhachi. A healthy diet of vitamins . . . meditation, and . . . weight lifting, . . . stretching and more stretching . . . all combined so that by the end of the summer (ten months after our first meditation healing session) Punchy could do one hundred full squats non-stop, walk five steps on his own, [and] walk behind his wheelchair with me sitting in it. . . .

The spirit of the lost. The practice of life. Peace Pilgrim, Soto monk, and former Vietnam gunship commander Claude An Shin Thomas writes: "Living in a culture of violence, we are conditioned to destroy and hate. We avoid our innermost thoughts and unknowingly contribute to the cycle of mistrust and rage. The world becomes our enemy and we lock ourselves into an encroaching spiral of self-destruction." Yet even in society's human penitential landfill of violence and fear a piece of bamboo can speak a deep reverence for life, can break the cycle of rage, and transform. These days one in every one hundred and fifty Americans is in one of these penitential landfills called a prison. What is wrong with this picture?

One of the worst moments of my life was when I stood at the locked door of the rehab facility in a small town in northwest Pennsylvania and watched my wife and children drive away. It wasn't by any stretch a jail, much less a maximum-security prison, but it was a kind of prison, a place where I had to give up ownership of my life as I had lived it; a place where doors locked and someone else had the key. What had I done to my life to get here? The shame was crippling. I couldn't blame or rage. I was crushed, defeated, felt barely human. It was a mild February day and the other patients were having their afternoon break outside, playing some sort of simple game with a soccer ball. I had to join them. Who were these people? How could I talk to them? Did they know how badly I had fucked up? I wanted to be alone. I wanted my family back. I wanted out. A black guy in a long brown overcoat limped up to me.

"You new?"

"Yes."

"My name's Ahmed. How you doin'?"

"I'm Terry. I feel like shit."

"Yeah, well, so does everyone else here. Where you from?"

And so we began talking. This stranger spoke as though there was nothing wrong with me—I was just another guy in trouble—but human. He restored my human dignity by his simple kindness. A bond was created in that moment. I have stood by it for ten years. Last I heard, Ahmed was in county lock-up in Charleston, South Carolina, for assault. In the past I have given him money even though "recovery" advocates and counselors urge against what they call enabling. I've bought him bus tickets, some of which he's used, some he's cashed. I've bailed him out of jail. I've tried to find him work. His beloved father died recently. His wife and kids left him years ago. He's a great con and will lie about anything if it will cover his butt or get him some drugs. His addiction governs his ability to decide about anything.

The roots of Ahmed's addiction go back thirty years. He also belonged to a radical black organization. He was at a university in the South and had his leg blown off in an accident where his "cell" had a munitions stash. Later some friends of his were killed or wounded in a shootout with local police. Both events made national headlines and set white people wondering fearfully if black revolutionaries were "everywhere." Ahmed went back to New York City, got a degree at Columbia, and entered the world of drugs for the easy money and the brief relief they provided from the constant pain in his stump.

When I first met him the addiction was not yet deep. He was doing rehab through a plea bargain instead of doing time for transporting drugs in his car. In rehab we talked and played cards and talked more. Ahmed played along with the counselors, saying all the right things, exercising his con skills. I was scared to death, really working the program, and didn't realize for years what he was up to. But I did encourage him to write his story down and he did that over the next six months or so. He has added to it over time. He is a natural storyteller. He created a strong cautionary drama out of his life in a style that would speak directly to anyone.

In the last chapter of "A View From the Inside," as he calls his story, he writes about the lowest point of his life when his crack addiction had him homeless, starving, and close to death. We had been out of touch for a few years. It was someone else who restored his humanity. He wrote:

> Thoughts of going home were long gone. I was now on a mission to stay high. I didn't call my job and I didn't call anyone in my family. I began to adapt to the lifestyle of a homeless crack addict. Abandoned buildings have no running water or electricity so I had to go outside and drink water from the fire hydrant in front of the building. I was real hungry but one hit of crack would take care of that, so I started my day with a couple of five dollar vials of crack and was immediately off to the races. This went on the whole day until I was completely out of money. How could I get more? I had to have more.
>
> I remembered the days I would drive the Cross Bronx Expressway to Jerome Avenue and at the end of the exit ramp there was always someone with a bucket of water and a rag to wipe off your car windows for a tip. I always gave them something because I concluded that it was better that they do this instead of robbing someone. I did not realize that except for the young boys, everyone else was doing it to buy crack. In a flash I was out there with them with a bucket and a rag. New York has a reputation of having some heartless people. However, many people would give me fifty cents or a dollar without me even wiping their windows. They probably figured I was homeless and needed to eat. Every time I would get ten dollars I would stop, go buy some crack, and sit in the park or a building and get high. This went on for four days

when God decided to remove me from this misery, since I had become incapable of doing it myself. One night as I sat on a car in front of the abandoned building, a tall Black male walked up and called his dog, "Mercenary! Come here!"

I said to myself, what an interesting name for a dog. A pit bull came running up and stood next to him at attention. He introduced himself as T-Ty and I told him that I bet I was the only one out there that knew what the name of the dog meant. With that he smiled and we began to talk. T-Ty was a Vietnam veteran and POW. He did two tours of Vietnam before being captured by the Vietnamese while on a mission deep in the jungle. He was a black belt in karate and a one-man fighting machine. After the war he became a soldier of fortune, that is, a hired mercenary, and saw action in many parts of the world, including Central America. What makes him unique is that he cares about other people.

After we finished talking, I realized that I hadn't slept in five days and was faced with the prospect of going in that building and having to close my eyes to get some sleep. I also had not taken my leg off and realized it was now in bad shape. I walked in the building to a back room and sat down on the couch. It was a cool summer night and I had on a short-sleeved shirt. There was no glass in the windows so the wind moved through the building unimpeded. I took my leg off, prayed to God, and closed my eyes.

About 6:30 a.m. I was awakened by T's voice, as he said, "I came to get you out of here." I began to cry as I thought about myself, my family, and the wretched state I was now in. I got up, put on my leg, and walked around the corner to the building that T-Ty rented a room in. He also used crack but was able to keep a roof over his head. He had a can of soup that he shared with me, and let me take a shower. I was able to keep my leg off the rest of the day as we talked and read the Bible.

It became clear to me that God had a plan and that I was not following it. I realized I had to take ownership of my actions and get the hell out of the Bronx. I got on the subway and headed to the Port Authority Bus Terminal. The corporate office for the bus company had an 800 number and, through the grace of God, I convinced someone in management to call the dispatcher and tell him to let me on the bus [to my dad's home in the Catskills] without a ticket. I was able to bring this merciless beating up of myself to an end.

He was okay for a while, then he started using again. He has been in and out of trouble and jobs many times since then. There is still the stigma around addiction that if a person were just strong enough they could beat the problem. That isn't how it works. Addiction is a disease that changes your body and your mind, your very metabolism. Once in the throws you cannot pretend you can go back physiologically or psychologically to how you were before. Somewhere between only 4 percent and 6 percent of those addicted ever recover from alcoholism, slightly higher percentages for other drugs. Not good odds and significant enough to point to something other than moral failure. This does not mean one reneges on responsibility for one's actions. Rather, one accepts responsibility in the context of an overpowering disease from which one cannot be healed without help and certainly not without scarring. I am not sure why I seem to have made it while others who have tried as hard have not.

So I do not judge Ahmed. When he calls he always says first, "Hey, brother!" And we are, beyond any bounds of race or blood. The gift of love is without time or scale. There have been times when my love for this brother was all he had. A decade ago his gift to me was life itself. How can I not be there for him now?

In Seed-Time Learn, in Harvest Teach, in Winter Enjoy

The old fools—
whatever it was they didn't know,
I don't want to know it either.
We are told to give away
what most we want
when all the evidence
says there is nothing to gain in giving.

Tableware and crockery transformed
light streaming across the afternoon
absolutely taking in every shadow and cry
returning just this
already and always.

At some point early in recovery and through intense zazen, the lies and fictions I had made of my life began to reveal themselves to me. As a boy I had learned my understanding of God was in all my actions. Turning from the truth of that experience, I thought I could own my life, direct it, force it to be one with my particular vision. Living with the complete but only partially apprehended being of my wife, I learned about loneliness in love. This seemed incomprehensible to me. I refused to see the arrogance of will, that the desire to make love a *thing*, a vision, rather than know it as an action of shared being was so much theater of the lost. Only when I arrived at the true cusp of loss, and there met others who had lost everything, did I begin to let go and by doing so begin to taste my own life as it was. My teachers have been many. A thousand subsequent lives would not be enough to thank them. And where is St. Nadie when I taste this life? St. Nadie is a habit of being, the habit of being when everything is stripped away, when you have nothing. If you are no one, you have nothing to lose, nothing to fear—only then can you be free enough to be open and caring for all things, only then begin to begin gratitude.

Part III

HELL IS BEING WITHOUT SPACE

6

GIVING UP WISDOM

A Zen practice with a beginning or an end is a contradiction. It is not a system or theory of belief but a means to escape the *need* for such a system or theory. If we want to live a life of open-hearted compassion, of peace of mind, we cannot just talk about it or merely want it; our manner of living must be different. We must experience it. We must express the experience by how we live.

Wittgenstein, that most aphoristic and quotable of modern philosophers, has said, "Philosophy is in fact the synopsis of trivialities." A summary of the worthless. How depressing; how exasperating. We want to exclude the trivialities, having valued them little or not at all. We want the big thing—the one true affirmation. We carry the wanting like a wound. We are like the thirsty man "who, in the midst of water, cries in thirst so imploringly."[1] What we get is a handful of fog or a burden of resentment that we try to manipulate into something meaningful, a certainty we are sure is out there, just beyond us, just at the edge of life—or death.

The city of Chillan, in south central Chile, lies in the breadbasket of that long, narrow country. Part of the year it is beset by seemingly endless rains, but the bounty of fruit and flowers in its open market, its mountains of blue squash and onions, its hillocks of tomatoes, its

1. D. T. Suzuki, *Manual of Zen Buddhism* (New York: Grove Press, 1960), 151.

symphonic thrum of hawking voices speak of rich soil, sufficient sun, and the life of family farms we no longer see in the States. It is a bit north of Temuco where Neruda was a boy, where Mistral taught school and wrote of poor women, and where hagiographers bring the future Nobel laureates together for a fateful meeting.

In Old Chillan ruins remain from an earthquake in the thirties in which tens of thousands were killed. Huge sycamores line the main streets, forming a green tunnel past parks, municipal buildings, and once prosperous houses.

On a roughly cobbled side street, behind a white wall with broken bottles on top, lies a *hospidaje*, a family run B&B. A retired couple have turned their home into a haven for travelers, a small walled-in patch of city property. The husband keeps bees. On both occasions we were there his wife warned us about the toilet and the water shortage, and he talked about his bees. He was like a servant in a temple, so reverential was he about them. He was deeply worried about some insect that had infested one hive and was impervious to the stings, an insect that was killing off the workers and the larvae. "They work so hard," he said, tears welling up, "that they die of exhaustion after a few weeks, maybe a month. Now this." He had two sets of hives, stacks of blue, red, yellow, and white boxes. His hand touched them tenderly as the little insects zipped in and out of the bottom slat of each. But he went on to show us the ripening fruit trees in his walled garden and the huge bunches of grapes in his arbor, under whose cool shade we sat. At breakfast we had fresh bread from the neighborhood bakery and his honey. His was a temple without doctrines. In his white suit and netted hat, with his smoke can in hand, he made a strange acolyte—but this was his practice from which he drew the experience of being, his walled patch of hospitality a hugeness that excluded nothing.

LULLABY OF THE BEEKEEPER OF CHILLAN

Even God sleeps now, my loves,
even failures and sin
snore alongside speech and truth,
but the bees do not sleep.

The grapes in the arbor sleep,
the old car in the back.
The lock in the gate sleeps,
the plum and cherry trees,
but the bees do not sleep.

The broom and the toilet sleep
and the old cobbles in the road.

The wife and the small grey birds sleep
and the bitter insect infesting the hive.
The door in its varnish sleeps,
but my bees do not sleep.

The stray dogs in the trash,
the wax sealed larvae sleep,
even the washing, the angels, the stars.
Things come and go,
but the bees do not sleep.

The Diamond Sutra says again and again that "all this fleeting world is a dream, a flickering lamp, a phantom . . ." What is a dream? Something we sense, perhaps even remember in detail, that is not "real"? Who walked there? Who spoke? We know it is not mere wishes—the *dream* of finding a perfect spouse; the *dream* of a better life, of happiness. Certainly some of our most deeply held wishes inform the dreams we experience asleep. We know they are not merely now somewhat discredited Freudian or Jungian symbols, in which water or light or color *represent* something other than what we experience in the dream, something masked, riddled, needing to be puzzled out by an expert. We know dreams are not only memories of a given day working themselves through our consciousness, perhaps even more muddled than when we engaged them awake. Nor are they visitations or messages from some other world or beings. Dreams are probably some mix of all these things, though I'm willing to let the idea of the messages go.

I had a dream once. In it there were several women and me, the only male. But before one dismisses it as another testosterone fantasy, I should say that in general I prefer the company of women to men. Most of my friends are women. Most of my colleagues at work are women. Women outnumber men in our sangha two to one, and even our abbot is a woman, though in her case she almost transcends gender. When my children were small and I cared for them at home, most of the adult people I encountered were women doing what I was doing. So it may not be wholly unusual that I meet more women than men in my dreams. It may be worth noting, however, that when I encounter Death in a dream, he is always male.

Novelist Robert Jordan has observed: "Men always believe they are in control of everything around them. When they find out they are not, they think they have failed, instead of learning a simple truth women already know." Perhaps it is a woman's tendency to accept the world rather than rule it that appeals to me. This was driven home at an all-day all-sangha meeting we held a few years ago. There had been crises at several Buddhist centers across the country, teachers abusing the power, intimacy, and trust with students—especially (but not exclusively) male teachers with female students. We wanted a chance to discuss these things freely among ourselves. The meeting was arranged so that we all, men and women, sat zazen together in the early morning, then had separate meetings for men and women the rest of the morning. The afternoon was to be a joint meeting, bringing the discussions together. No great things emerged by the end of the day, save for a new and deeper, slightly amused (for the women) and chagrined (for the men) perception of how the genders handle complex and subtle issues differently.

The men were very earnest and caring. They examined and analyzed the problems as they saw them, weighing evidence and moral imperatives against spiritual authority. They felt it was important to "help our Dharma sisters" by supporting them in their vulnerability and assisting in a *solution* for the problem as regards our sangha in particular. We had a goal and we reached for it. When we joined the women in the afternoon, we were ready to report.

The women did not have a report. They listened patiently to ours and some of the women, those accustomed to dealing with men at work, made responses that seemed, at first sniff, like reasoned ones by individuals who had been paying attention to the report. But they were really just polite efforts not to dismiss us altogether. The conversation resumed—for that is what the women had been doing all morning, conversing, bringing things up, putting some on the table, discarding others, no solution sought, no resolution needed, no particular goal. Our male presumption was an embarrassment.

In my dream I was in a grassy meadow in a lovely park. I was standing at a wooden podium and there were several large easy chairs spread around on the grass in front of me. I was trying very hard to explain something. Women of varying ages, shapes, and sizes occupied the chairs. The dream took its own direction away from me.

Myo-On Maurine Stuart, a teacher to my teacher and from whom I received the Precepts in a *Jukai* ceremony, had a favorite word— *wonderful.* She always said it *wonder-full.* Her teaching was that the wonder is making space out of no-space, out of "other" to "all." On her deathbed, ending a long struggle with cancer, her last words were: "Oh, great peace. Nobody there!" Not nobody else, but no one at all.

Auden says somewhere that a young woman should be suspicious when a boyfriend starts sending her love poems because, while he may still love her, while he is writing he is thinking *about* his love for her and not actively loving her. Likewise, when Bertrand Russell could not make sense out of Wittgenstein's thought, he tried to appeal to some fact *about* Wittgenstein that would make Wittgenstein's having such thoughts more intelligible. He could only explain what was incomprehensible to him; he couldn't make sense of it, nor get inside it. We select meaning we find useful in an evolutionary way, a matter of natural selection rather than objective truth.

In the film π (*pi*), a number theorist encounters Kabala numerologists. They want him to tell them that the 216 digit number that will reveal the true name of God. He says he can't, that it's inside him, that besides it is not a number, it is the "syntax, the spaces between the numbers."

In chapter fifteen of the Tao Te Ching it is written:

> The ancient Masters were profound and subtle.
> Their wisdom was unfathomable.
> There is no way to describe it;
> All we can describe is their appearance.[2]

"There is nothing like reality," a friend tells me. Our poverty of knowing is so great we are afraid to admit to it, but we would rather blather and rationalize our way away, as though by pretending to know

2. Stephen Mitchell, *Tao Te Ching* (New York: Harper Collins, 1988).

who we are we can leave our mark on the world. What then when the mark we leave is a wound?

I have been occupied with what we can know, and with how we hurt others by our actions, for some time. Twenty years ago, in my first book of poems, *Cambios*, based on daily readings in the I Ching, I wrote many poems that explored these themes, even as my addiction was beginning to take hold. I found no answers, but only experiences of being human, confused, anxious to love and be loved, to make a mark and to be, at the same time, invisible, all the while bearing the burden of whatever I did.

From Cambios

CXXV

We gave up sainthood and wisdom
to know our place, to burn a little, to be still
and so master the restless wind.
It comes from fire,
a sign of mystery
and a sign of the family.
It merges with dust
to become visible.

CXXV *Chia Jen* (family, clan)

CCLXXXVIII

Constellations are stillness,
the miscellaneous distance of stars
racing away, the lie of light,
one form of sight.
Who contemplates the forms,
the shapes, the changes of time
or perhaps the forms of men
holding hard to bony ways,

the world thought of,
has also the sense
without an explanation of it.

CCLXXXVIII *Pi* (grace)

7

THE THIEF IN THE INFINITY OF CHILDHOOD

Landscape seems to most of us a timeless, permanent thing. Mountains are often used as metaphors for eternity. Gnarled old wolf-maples experience human generations as we would experience a year. Or as we said as kids, they experience a year as a day. But this, as we also know in another part of our minds, is not really the case. Not far from where I am sitting is a pair of merimictic lakes, not very wide but very deep indeed (400+ feet). They are holes drilled into soft clay deposits by cataracts that poured off the mile-high face of the receding glaciers of the last Ice Age, a mere fifteen thousand years ago. This timeless-seeming landscape of rolling forested hills did not even exist when the lakes were being formed. In the many shale-filled gorges near the moraines and "Finger Lakes" throughout the region are fossil deposits from the saline sea. It once covered this land of settled dairy farms and villages that make up a once prosperous but now poverty-stricken countryside. Barns, less than a century old, are everywhere sagging into the ground. Sometimes the wood is sold off to designers and decorators in New York City for clients who want that "authentic" country look. What they do not recognize is that the wood represents a lost way of life that seemed as solid as the earth itself. Rusted tractors, plows, harrows, corn-pickers stand in fallow fields.

The land where the lakes lie was once a farm of 1,500 acres. It was settled in 1816, expanded from 500 acres of the Military Tract, bought on the cheap from some soldier in the Continental Army. His pay had been land in the Tract, millions of acres of wilderness, from a Treasury that had no cash but lots of land. He and other Revolutionary soldiers quickly sold off their land wages for hard cash. The Collin family, which arrived in the hard winter of 1816–17, saw only forest of centuries old trees to be conquered. They lived on that land for 170 years. I was with the last of the line when she died. Now it is State Park and suburban tracts. Actually, things began to unravel after only eighty years. One of David Collin's daughters contested his will and the ensuing courtroom drama split the family as well as the farm irreparably. Yet they were considered one of the "old" families in their town. All gone now.

The Onondaga people are not the first humans to occupy this land, but they have been here close to a thousand years. It was only five or six hundred years ago, around the time of Chaucer, that Dekanawidah, the Peacemaker, crossed Lake Ontario in his white stone canoe and met with Ayenwatha to bring the five original Iroquois nations together under the sacred White Pine. Their empire lasted nearly as long as Rome's, covering much of the Northeast and into what is now Canada, until the Jesuits and the British came, like the Huns, and divided their ancient trusts. The nobility of those who remain true to those trusts, their connectivity to this place, is deep and wonderful to behold. But it is not so ancient to be beyond reckoning. It has its roots in a discoverable past.

When I was at school in England I read Chaucer for the first time in the Middle English. I was moved and charmed by the palpable texture of the language, the feel of the words over my tongue, and with the music of the verse I saw colors, both bright and earthy. At six hundred years, it is a language barely intelligible today, unlike Shakespeare's, which at four hundred is wholly available to us:

> Whan that Aprill with his shoures soote
> The droughts of March hathe perced to the roote

And bathed every veyne in swich licour
Of which vertu engendered is the flour

I sensed even then that this was the language of my consciousness. When the wind was in a "swough" I could hear and feel it roaring through the temple of Mars in the "Knyght's Tale." Inspired by this new sense of identity with an author, I took a bus, one Saturday off, to nearby Canterbury to see the cathedral and the Shrine. I was awed by many things—the tomb of the Black Prince, the sixth-century throne of the English St. Augustine who founded the first monastery at the site, the soaring vaults, the crypts—and I felt the usual things an American boy might feel when confronted with the work of the ages. But at one point I stood on the stone where tradition has it St. Thomas à Beckett was slain. I stood there alone. Sixteen. When Chaucer's pilgrims arrived there it was already three hundred years old, older than my own nation, and *that* visit was six hundred years before I arrived, another pilgrim. I felt a flow of eons like tides moving back and forth through me. Though the nearly thousand-year span was only a moment in the history of man and the history of man barely a blink in the history of the planet, the barriers and distances vanished, the tides were vast and their pull caught each cell. Where do *you* go? Where do you come from? In that moment there was no coming or going. How could there be any *where*?

Landscapes change profoundly through time. So do we. What change could be more profound than death?

I am at an age when people I know die. Parents, grandparents, friends. No matter how prepared I think I am, mortality is always a surprise. I look at the shock, the soul-bruising hurt in the faces of friends who have lost someone. Who dies? What goes? What remains? Am I next? For most of us, in the beginning, death and all the complex fears attached to it make up our hell. Death so suffocatingly takes away all our space, all our hope, makes tomorrow seem empty and the past so brief we wonder if it ever was. It is the thief that invades the infinity of childhood and removes everything. There are four deaths that have changed me and, in a way, through them I learned some answers. But the answers we learn through death are often to questions we haven't even asked yet.

One evening, a week after I turned five, my mother called me into the little kitchen of the bungalow we were renting. My dad was there but he was looking out the window. She sat me down and said she had something to tell me. My eyes shot back and forth between them. I was suddenly scared. Then she said, "The angels have come and taken Granpop away." That is all I recall. Just that. If there were other words, they are lost. For a few seconds I was numb, trying to take in what it meant. Then, even though I could not understand that he was dead— dead did not mean anything real for some years yet—I realized I would never see him again. Gone. Zip. Vanished. Who were these angels? How or why could they? I disintegrated, howling they had to bring him back. I felt my mother's arms around me. I cried so hard my head felt pins and needles against the cloth on her breast. It went on for a long time. Something was torn out of me, something real.

Can there be soul mates fifty years apart? What strange conjunction of events brought these two unlikely beings together: my grandfather the lush, the dreamer, the sweet-talker, the brilliant painter who never saw anything major through to completion, and me, the wide open boiling boy? Each year now, for forty-six years, on August 15, even when I've forgotten the date, I feel a strange aching, like an old wound acting up. My teacher Shinge Roshi has noted that many people who come to Zen have experienced such traumatic loss at an early age. From this death I learned who I was: alive, mortal, breakable, wounded, lost, alone, wonder-full.

Many, many years later, when I was a parent myself, I received a phone call from my dad. His mother had just died, apparently peacefully in her own home, aged ninety-two. Somewhere Robert Bly says a man doesn't grow up until his father dies. That may be true for many men, but I didn't begin to grow up until Gran Marie died. I recall turning away from the grave when an uncle, notable for his histrionics, broke down, unable to contain any longer the hugeness of my own loss in the face of his grief. What I grieved at her death was not the loss of all the nostalgic things: her amazing cooking, her funny Czech-accented English (scrambellied eggs), the smell of her house, her delicate gardens, the glint of humor in her almost black eyes. Nor was it the wisdom I would no longer hear: "Why do you want to be like everybody else? You're *you*!" (This said to me in my teens when I responded to criticism of my clothes by saying everyone else was wearing them.) Nor did I grieve the dissolution of the family, that loose amalgam of selfish oddballs held together around an invisible center by her life-force, now spinning wildly away (we never see one another any more). What I grieved was her. She was the only one from whom I ever experienced unconditional love. She was my model for being whole in the world. Now I had to let go and learn on my own. From this death I learned that I needed to grow up and what that meant.

My dad died before he was seventy, after a long and painful decline. Officially it was kidney failure that brought him down, twisted in agony, half off his hospital bed.

In truth it was decades of hard drinking and smoking, and a blind physical, almost self-inflicted punishment in work—that masculine "hard knocks" approach to personal health that often masks a kind of death wish. We were not close, though we wanted to be. There was one occasion, a year or so before his actual death, when we thought he wasn't going to make it. Neither did he. He could barely talk, but from the bed, amid tubes, catheters, dialysis machines, he uttered, "I love you." Something he never actually said to me before that I could recall in the forty-odd years of my life then. Instead of joy at finally hearing those longed-for words, I was bitter at what seemed a ridiculous deathbed conversion. When he did die, I wasn't there. No one was. Alone. In unbelievable pain, the life of this fiercely gentle, hard-working man ended. At the funeral I read from Thomas's "Do Not Go Gentle into That Good Night." There were many people. His brothers, friends, all in tears. I had none, until I came to these lines:

> And you, my father, there on the sad height,
> Curse, bless me now with your fierce tears I pray.

From this death I learned that what I wanted was to forgive.

Betsy Knapp was the last of the Collin family. She came from what she called "good stock," a family important from before the American Revolution. I came to know her when I was in grad school. I had to do some field work for my master of library science (MLS) and she needed someone to help with her family archives. She seemed ferocious when she spoke to our class, scaring off the fools and the faint of heart, I suppose. But there was something about her directness I liked, so I volunteered. Over the years she became an honorary aunt to my children and for them the Christmas season didn't really begin until we went to Betsy's to cut our tree and enjoy the annual party with hot cider, cocoa, and endless plates of German Christmas cookies by the fire.

Betsy was diabetic. In her last couple of years, I went over once a week, ostensibly to work with her on her family history, but actually to clean up the mess she had made as she'd fade in and out of insulin problems, and also to keep her company in the long chats over figures in her family's past. After her last stroke I went to see her every day in the hospital. I had to feed her because the nurses merely left the food on a tray for her, but her mouth had become so swollen from drying out and her grip on eating utensils so tenuous she was getting more food on her chest than in her mouth. Hospice got her to her home when it was clear the end was coming. She had held on so she could go home to die in the very room her father died in.

The last day was a wild February day. Massive, pounding winds sounded like all the spirits of the place were roaring around the house. She was the last and her tough affection had taught us all about the power of love and land. Though unconscious, she knew we were present, myself and Antje Lemke, her former longtime companion and the one great love of her life. Antje held her old head in her arms. The wind picked up, almost screaming in the eaves. Betsy's breathing changed, then changed again, slowed, and stopped. Despite the winds, a silence filled us all. We were sad, but also there was such loving in the little room that we could let go. The grief was real, deep, but gentled by an unconditional loving we had earned from one another. From this death I learned what I had become.

The Hours of Folly Are Measured by the Clock but of Wisdom No Clock Can Measure

Death tells all which is nothing.
Close to the dangerous borders
you look around.
It is still there,
the clamoring of what you missed,
the skin of time
crumpled like roadkill,
your lists of omissions.

The granddaughter of reason
has deceived you
among the upper and lower skies,
the old house across the marshes,
the instruments and papers
scattered about the maw of the earth.
Even when facts are worse than suspicions
the suspicions are worse.

You thought you were great
because your remoteness was great
but now you open even as you die,
peddling last words for each moment.
You eat not because you're hungry
but because you're alive.
Go fight with your worms.

8

NO BLAME

I am neither a scholar nor a philosopher, a thing which is by now obvious to anyone reading this who is also a professional in those fields. I read a lot. I keep a commonplace book and sometimes remember to write down the citation of whatever point or phrase it was that caught my attention. It is no bibliography or index so much as a jog to a fallible memory. This commonplace book is necessary because I cannot possibly remember everything I read, yet I am usually convinced as I write something down that I will recall whence it came. I rarely do. I've kept one since I was sixteen. Certain things do stick in my head, disparate things that somehow make sense together, scraps of ideas, odd bits of someone else's intuition or insight, old rock songs.

There's an old Guy Clark tune about this kid and an aging drifter who takes him up. It is superficially about the wisdom learned on the road, in bars and pool halls—but it is also about desperation, wanting something *out there* to save us from our terrible empty mortality, if we could only discover it, managing instead the temporary fix of drugs, alcohol, or the one-night stand. A counselor I know says that the insidious thing about drugs and alcohol is that they work, they do exactly what we want them to do . . . for a while; then they kill us. The refrain of the Clark song goes, "We're like desperados waiting for a train." It often runs through my head when I confront my own wanting. I hear it when I look at others wishing, waiting, hoping on some dry hillside of their spirit for that sound, that rumble on the tracks, the answer at last, rubbing raw again and again the bitterness that is there when it doesn't come. Who among us hasn't felt the gritty winds of longing? Who hasn't sat poised, hopeless?

Where does disappointment take you? If it happens often enough it leads to anger, an inchoate resentment. Someone has *got* to be to blame for this situation. Maybe it's us. Maybe we will deny it is us, even when we suspect it is us, and we'll turn the self-loathing the ensuing resentment generates upon others. Anger. Blame. So pervasive are they in the bones of human culture. Road rage. Children slaughtering children. Someone screws up at work and we fire him instead of going after the problem. Who's to blame?

A theater troupe in my town, the Open Hand Theater, runs the International Puppet and Mask Museum. In their collection is a wooden helmet mask from West Africa, which has a carved snake surrounding it. The snake is not there as a symbol of evil, as we might construe it in the West. It is there because it sheds its skin and renews itself, leaving the old skin behind. In the community of its origin there is a ceremony for when a member of the community commits a crime or major transgression against it. The individual is compelled to wear the mask and in doing so becomes the snake. He or she is allowed to shed his or her skin of the old life. All that went on is left behind and forgotten, dead. Life begins anew. What is powerful about this is that the whole community participates. Everyone shares in this rebirth, in this leaving behind. They collectively forget the individual's old skin, old life of error, and accept the new person as one of them, giving him or her a new name. One is given a second chance. The past is dead. There is no blame.

Is this possible for us, in a world where an "eye for an eye" has for so long been a way of life that it is a reflex? Can we really drop the burden of resentment? Where does the bitterness of thwarted dreams and expectations appear most profoundly but in families? It is said family members can push your buttons better than anyone else because they installed them. This is true among siblings. This is true between couples. Some years ago my wife and I nearly ended our marriage. We are from a generation in which half of once married couples are divorced. The twenty-four years we had managed at that point were a kind of record among many of our acquaintances. But we had come to an end point. It was impossible to continue as we were.

Four years before I had complained to my alcoholism counselor that I could stop drinking, would at least drink less, if my marriage were in better shape, if certain things changed. He said no real changes could happen until I took alcohol out of the equation, because whenever anything went wrong we would never be able to look at the real issues. Alcohol would always be in the way, an excuse or scapegoat. So I had been in recovery four years. I was making real progress toward changing my life, but *we* were not. It is not that my wife was not also working toward change. But as a couple all the old behaviors were still in place and we had no tools to change them, to even see what needed to change. Once again we sought help. We were caught in the complex web of codependence, almost a clichéd term these days, layers of knotted, tangled anger, distancing, reconciliation, unutterable loneliness, total dependence of one's feelings on how the other felt. There seemed no way out. There seemed so many real reasons to blame the other, neither of us could enter the fields of compromise any longer. We felt we had compromised our lives away. Somewhere love had gotten lost in the tangle.

Perhaps it was the sad aftertaste of love lost that led us to counseling again. Perhaps the echoes of pure joy we had in discovering one another during those young years still rang somewhere inside us. For whatever reason, we didn't quite give up. Our counselors (we drew on several resources: family therapy, our spiritual teacher, AA, and Alanon) taught us a great deal. Three things come particularly to mind:

1. *Shut up and listen.* So preoccupied were we by our own noise we never heard one another.

2. *Stop, pause, examine what happened.* This was a very artificial thing to do at first, to put aside righteous anger and look at what had happened to make us angry. She would, for example, make what was to her some innocuous comment about money. I would immediately tense up, wondering what she might mean. A touchy issue between us. She always made much more than I and wouldn't trust me with my own checkbook for years. I was reluctant, of course, to admit I had been unreliable. I had to ask for grocery money, a humiliating situation many women who are homemakers find themselves in. Her insecurity about my recovery added to the problem, as did my sensitivity to her insecurity. She in fact asked, when she visited me in rehab, if after what we had to pay for the rehabilitation, since insurance didn't cover it, I could guarantee I would stop drinking. It made me feel that it was the money that mattered, not my recovery. Eventually I felt inferior, stupid when it came to anything regarding money. So when the topic came up, even in a minor way, even though we both thought we were past those behaviors, all this baggage came with it. I was hopelessly hypersensitive. Reason had nothing to do with it. My "trigger" was cocked, ready to fire at the least suggestive change in tone of voice, a few ill-chosen words, a look I could interpret as critical regarding money. And once having started off with an angry response and feeling the energy escalate, to have to pause and examine what happened, to explain my paranoia about money, my guilt, my inferiority, to actually discover it as we talked, was hugely difficult. But it was the beginning of listening, of discovering how we misunderstood each other and assigned motives where there were none.

3. *No blame.* This was the most powerful and resonant of all. One day we were sitting with Shinge Roshi, seeking her

advice. We were both her students, fond of her, committed to the practice. She had had a lot of experience, both personal and as a counselor, with the vicissitudes of marriage. We took turns complaining about various things. Suddenly she stopped us. "I want both of you to sit with 'No Blame'! Just No Blame. Not don't you blame her, or don't you blame him. Not don't blame your past, or your drinking, or your sex lives. Just no blame. Take blame out of the equation. What does it mean to have a life with no blame?"

And that is the question. What does it mean? It means the Holocaust victim refuses to hate the Germans because the hatred would make him like them. It means the Dalai Lama feels grief for the Chinese because of the genocide they have committed on his people. It means that Thich Nhat Han can, in "Call Me by My True Name," feel love for a pirate who rapes and kills a child as well as grief and love for the suffering and loss of the child. It means that ordinary people can let go of the past and forgive. It means we deny nothing, that we give ourselves away without ceasing, that we admit everything into our hearts, hearts that are, as my daughter once said when she was quite small, "SO big!"

In Japan there is a custom called *Osaki-ni.* It is a kind of deep courtesy in which one apologizes for the grief one can cause another. It is especially so in cases over which we have no control, such as death. You know your parting will cause others sorrow, and you thus express your sorrow at having to be the first to go. In it blame vanishes. We do not mistake certain loves, and when we stand in the wake of another's death we do not blame them for dying. Deep courtesy goes both ways.

The *Tao Te Ching* says, "The enemy is a shadow you yourself cast." The shadow wanders our unregarded hours where we hold resentments, where we are lost, when there is nothing and no one to blame, though we keep on blaming. I often wonder what is the light that hits the ego, casting out the shadow? It is gratitude. And if the ego is gone, as it is when we are truly grateful, there is *no one* to cast a shadow. We can replace blame with gratitude—in any circumstance. Blame builds up walls around the self and points only outward. Gratitude opens the heart, dissolves the self, and points everywhere.

There is a moment at the close of Jane Kenyon's poem "Chrysanthemums" that expresses this experience. Her husband, Donald Hall, also a poet and a rather older man, had just barely survived major surgery. She sat with him through the worst, watching him make his way back to life. There was much to worry and complain about. With staples removed and discharge papers in hand, she drives him home:

> . . . he dozed in the car
> woke, and looked with astonishment
> at the hills, gold and quince
> under October sun, a sight so
> overwhelming that we began to cry,
> first he, and then I.

The couplet closing the poem is so poignant, pulling us along into her opening of gratitude and wonder, that miracles are available to any of us and that they are not what we expect them to be. "No blame" does not stand alone. It requires gratitude. When we forget to be grateful we are only half alive.

Lullaby of Osaki-ni

Who loves the pilgrim
and the changing face,
the first look of the shadows?
Who stoops over your bed,
who eases your whimpering?
Who bears the day burdens
into evening,
who is half lost in gathering night?
Had we been young together
you would know
the grey wind and the stars
turn in the wake.

9

BE KIND

The Dalai Lama, when asked what it takes to be a good Buddhist, simply replies, "Be kind." On the surface this seems too easy, like saying, "Be a nice guy." We can all manage that from time to time. But if you sit with this *be kind* and probe what it means to *be* kind, then the resonance of the phrase grows infinite.

Be kind to others? Sure.

To yourself? Maybe. But how to do it without being selfish?

To animals? Of course—they are our brothers and sisters.

To trees and plants? They are also our brothers and sisters.

How about things? How can you be kind to a toilet or the dirt you've swept off the kitchen floor? By keeping the one clean and handling the other mindfully, knowing *fully* what it is.

Nothing left out, nothing superfluous, nothing wasted.

We have all been surprised by acts of kindness to us, seeming to come out of nowhere just at the crucial moment. I recall teaching one night at the Rome (NY) extension of Mohawk Valley Community College. It was winter. Students stayed past the 9:30 p.m. end of class to chat and ask about papers due. It was well after 10 when I began the twenty-mile drive home over snowy country roads. About two miles out of the city I had a flat. When I got out of the car I gasped a little. It was about 10 degrees and the wind was whipping snow ghosts across the empty road and the exposed, frozen fields. I fumbled getting the hatchback open for the spare and the tire iron, only to find the spare flat too. I put the flashers on and walked about a quarter mile to the nearest farmhouse, hoping to make a call for help. The house was dark and silent, but I knocked anyway, figuring folks would help in an emergency, and anyone knocking at the door at this hour was in trouble. No answer. I walked to the next place, another quarter mile further on. Same non-response. I was getting pretty cold, but there was nothing for it. I had to carry the spare the, now, two and a half miles back to Rome and find either a phone or an all-night service station to mend it. Walking along into the wind, shifting the frozen, heavy tire from arm to arm, I was feeling tired and very sorry for myself. The whole time out there I hadn't seen one car.

Then lights did indeed appear behind me. A car was approaching. A station wagon drove by. I couldn't even get my thumb out in time to beg a ride. But it stopped. Back-up lights came on and the driver headed in reverse to me. He rolled down the window, "Looks like you could use some help?"

"Yeah, a flat. And the spare's flat too."

"Look, throw the tire in the back on top of that stuff and hop in."

I was frozen. I didn't hesitate. The back of the wagon was full of sales samples of some sort. We drove into Rome and cruised awhile, looking for an all-night service station. When we found one, I thanked my lift, but he just said he'd wait and see how it went. The guys in the service station didn't have much to do after 11 p.m., so they patched up the tire quickly and refused to charge me for it. My salesman then drove me back out of the city to my car and sat in his by the roadside, headlights trained on my flat, while I changed it. He coached me a little too, saying I should put the tire iron on so it was parallel to the ground and to then stomp on it to loosen the frozen nuts, and to do the same on the other side to tighten them again. Before too long it was done. My hands were cut, raw, throbbing, but I put one out to shake his.

"Say, you ought to tell me your name so I can thank you properly."

"My name doesn't matter. But you can do this for me. The next time you see someone in trouble on the road, you stop and help them. Then we'll be even. Goodnight."

He rolled up his window, but he waited until my car started up and then we drove off in opposite directions. That is one sort of kindness—toward others.

Shortly after I got out of rehab I was talking with an old drinking buddy, also on the wagon, the sort of guy who got into fights in bars when people criticized "dumb Micks," thereby only proving the criticism. I was saying that I had gone to rehab for my kids so they wouldn't have ruined childhoods with their old man a lush. He grabbed me by the arm, all kidding suddenly aside:

"If you think you are doing this for someone else, you're headed for trouble. You'll be back again in a few months. You've *got* to learn that you have to do this for *you*! If you're sick you'll be no good to anyone anyway. You have to take care of yourself first."

Coming from him this was a shock. I'd heard something similar in rehab, of course, but didn't really get it. I'd been taught as a boy that putting yourself first was unmanly, cowardly. Real men would rather die than be thought selfish. My friend made that sound banal and stupid. He was talking about another sort of kindness—toward oneself.

What is kindness? Completeness. Imagine being kind without discrimination. Kindness is like faith, you cannot pretend to be it. There is the "fake it till you make it" practice, but you must be aware you are faking it and that to really make it or be it you must earn it. Kindness is not given to you, though you experience it from others. I believe we are led to kindness through Great Compassion, which I understand to be a deep comprehension of mortality, what it means to live. My practice of kindness is gratitude. I express it through bowing. We do a lot of bowing in Zen circles—to our teacher, the zendo, the altar (a reminder that an ordinary man achieved insight), our sitting cushions, one another. Of course, it is a carryover from the Asian traditions, but it is useful to learn what it can mean for us rather than merely mimicking habit.

The first time I served as *jikijitsu*, the meditation leader, I had to bow in front of everyone at the brief ceremony at the close of the last sitting. I stood there behind the bowing mat in the center of the zendo, two neat rows of students on either side of me in deep silence. I realized I was bowing for them, with them, and for and with all students ever. I wept as I bowed, flooded with an inexpressible gratefulness for the simple chance to be thankful.

In his wonderful and justly famous book *Zen Mind, Beginner's Mind*, Shunryu Suzuki Roshi gives us permission to experience everything anew. One might ask why we need permission, but such experience requires a total surrender. Who will do that willingly? A young woman who began to sit with the small meditation group I lead at the University's chapel told me of an experience she had. We sat on the chapel steps, feeding crumbs from our sandwiches to sparrows. Normally, she says, her head feels like a rock, so heavy she can't keep it up. After a more recent sitting, she told me she felt like she had no head at all. Everything was light, white, and floating. She was filled with peace and joy. Then she felt a tear hit her chin and she became aware of her experience. She pulled out of it and began to think *about* it instead of continuing to experience it directly. She was angry with herself at once for pulling away and for thinking that maybe the experience was somehow false, which is perhaps why she instinctively pulled away.

Astronaut Story Musgrave once told me how he likes, when the other Space Shuttle crewmembers are asleep in their bags, to push himself off his pallet and suspend himself floating weightless and motionless in the shuttle to sleep. He says his mind opens completely and unrestrainedly, that the conditions of the body—what he calls the natural gravity vector orientation—vanish and any sense of a physical *you* vanishes too. He is there and everywhere at once. He says he has learned to experience this any place now, not just in space. He can do it because he trusts the experience, knows it is real, and surrenders to the reality.

Trust is not belief. Love is not hope. To be open is to be kind. It ceases to be a question of choice. It is simply good. We comprehend our comprehender. As you cannot decide to be kind or compassionate, you cannot summon this sort of grace on your own. You have to trust it is there and open to it. This is another sort of kindness—to surrender, to be open, to trust.

Shame Is Pride's Cloak

Anger, greed, sorrow, pride—
just possibilities that haunt
because they are not whole;
the implications of time and space,
not crows and small birds in the morning,
not the grey wind nor the gold.

Unbodied speech and disappointments,
exquisite clues
to everything you use
to become unlovable.
Once again you fail.

Bow with humility, bow with rage.
Bow to the one
who bows before the wind.
Lift up your voice and plead for all.

10

LOVE EVERYTHING

I read somewhere that the monotheist's God is an angry god because he has to do everything alone. I think this sense of an angry god is why we are often angry, though we may not know it is why. We are so tired of being alone. We want to be loved, nurtured, understood. One of the world's great paradoxes that I have experienced but do not understand is that it is precisely what you want that you should give away. Somehow it comes back manyfold: money, time, love.

It takes courage to love without expectation or even thought of return, without conditions. Usually, when I want someone to love me, as Iris Murdoch points out so lucidly, I want them to love *me*, not some abstract intrinsic nature of me. We are trapped by what Gerard Manley Hopkins called "the pitches of suchness"—the degrees of value or comparison. We are afraid to lose ourselves even while we know we must. We are afraid of the mystery of love, substituting too often the certainty of desire. Mystery for most people is an interesting uncertainty, something not quite understood. But in love we want to take out the uncertainty. When we do, the mystery goes with it, along with the interest. For a Buddhist love is an incomprehensible certainty.

How do we encompass this unconditional hugeness? The "Poet of the Prairie," William Least Heat-Moon, says, "Only horizon and sky are given up easily. Take the numbing distance in small doses and gorge on the little details that beckon." And we should, at the same time, as

Linda Gregg suggests, "sing as if the sky were listening." Even Tolkien has written: "He had never before been able to walk into the distance without turning it into mere surroundings . . . [then he found] you could go on and on and have a whole country in a garden."

For love is action. It is not saying or wishing or hoping or longing. And it is in the details. I notice that I love my wife—am filled with my love for her, not by thinking of or desiring her, but by watching her move across a room, catching the tender magic as she handles pie-dough, or as she drifts idly in a canoe, trailing her hand in the water, watching her being in the world in her own small-self way.

In a letter Georgia O'Keefe wrote: "It takes time to see, like to have a friend takes time." We absolutely must give ourselves time to love. In loving one unconditionally, we come to love all. As O'Keefe also writes: "I had nothing but to walk into nowhere and the wide sunset space with the stars." As Soen Roshi loved to point out, "nowhere" is also "now here." Further, there are no witnesses to unconditional love, giving and receiving unfrought with meaning.

Everything Possible to be Believed Is an Image of Truth

For the moment cars have stopped passing
on the main road.
Cold crackles the very air
over the whole city.
A window unlearns itself
and the full winter moon
rises over the blue neighborhoods.
It does not change anything.

There is no need to remind the universe you are here. Without conditions, how could it matter? This is the fear we pair with love, that love will not matter, that *we* will not matter. How can we be centered in that uncaring hugeness? Inertia and monotony are the result of fear. Former poet-laureate Robert Haas speaks of this in regard to Basho and Vermeer: "The extraordinary thing . . . about Basho's poems or Vermeer's paintings is that the world is not set against any particular loss or peril to give it intensity or importance, and they do not will into the world any more loss or peril than all of us must suffer as a condition of being alive." Great Compassion in action. Any part of the world completely seen is the world. When we come to glimpse *being* in this way no one is surprised by the fullness and the emptiness of things. Again O'Keefe, that long-lived woman who lived alone in the vast empty desert yet who wrought paintings with such loving detail exploded into vastness that they speak to everyone, writes: "My center does not come from my mind. It feels in me like a plot of warm moist well-tilled earth with the sun shining hot on it. . . . It seems I would rather feel it starkly empty than let anything be planted that cannot be tended to the fullest possibility of its growth. . . ." So we must begin loving everything by loving ourselves.

With breath we begin and end life. With breath we feel another breathing next to us. There are no thoughts attached. We just do it. Can you not also feel the breath that is more deeply in you than you are yourself? It is love. Breathe it and you breathe everything.

Things aren't supposed to happen according to plan. Plans are conditional. We learn this from John Ashberry, who writes: "It is the lumps and trials / and whether we shall be known / and whether our fate can be exemplary like a star." Who does not know the burden of living or the debilitating burden of pain? Even as a child I worried about the sadness of things, that the purpose, meaning, value of each little thing would be lost. This is not an uncommon attitude in children. Arnold

Lobel has a story called "Tearwater Tea" in which his owl begins to think of chairs with broken legs, things lost behind furniture, broken toys, forks missing tines. The terrible sadness of the lost, broken, and forgotten things brings the owl to tears. The tears fill a kettle and he brews it up for tea. A very refreshing tea!

Remembering things, remembering people, knowing them attentively, mindfully, where and as they are—a sadness and a wonder with no blame, kindly, lovingly. Murdoch writes: "Metaphysics and human sciences are made impossible by the penetration of morality into the moment to moment conduct of ordinary life: the understanding of this fact is religion (it makes nonsense of all your solipsistic sophisms). . . . There is no beyond, there is only here, the infinitely small, infinitely great and utterly demanding present."

Shakyamuni, the historical Buddha, and Lao Tzu arrived independently at the same understanding of nothingness, or *shunyata*. We should not dismiss it because it is an ancient discovery that came to us as new only recently. Its late arrival in our cultural consciousness has more to do with our own intellectual and spiritual xenophobia than with the validity of the insight. Humanity is not necessary. Nor are we the measure of what is true.

> "Here is a solution to the problem of creation which is new to Western philosophy: the universe can arise out of nothing because non-existence itself is not characterless or negative. . . . [H]ere is a metaphysical system which starts not with matter or with ideas, but with Law (Tao), non-existence and existence as the three fundamental categories of reality. . . . After Parmenides declared that non-existence cannot exist, Western philosophers never attempted to challenge his dogma. The non-being of Plato and Plotinus, like the empty space of Greek atomists, was given no positive character. Only Einsteinian space-time—which is nothing, yet directs

the motion of particles—comes at all close to Lao-Tsu's concept of non-existence."[3]

However we may imagine this statement to apply to life, it does not, for example, penetrate the cycles of poverty or addiction in which people find themselves, nor can we ever force, with an act of sheer will, this reality to transform our situation. Nothingness remains a concept. I thought I could think my way out of my addiction. If I could just understand it deeply enough I would be able to drink again safely. It's like trying to think your way out of diabetes or, for that matter, Graves' Disease.

During one counseling session in rehab I tried to talk my way through my thinking about it. In exasperation my counselor threw up his hands and came within inches of my face. He spoke slowly and firmly, "If you're so fucking smart, what are you doing here?" I had, of course, no answer. I had made a mess of things. I had to sit, listen, and re-learn how to live. There is no recovery pill. Life can only speak life. An alcoholic cannot think his way out of his disease; he has to live his way out. Intellect cannot supersede itself. Intellect raises the questions, but it cannot answer them. It is life itself that resolves them. One has to be open to it, allow it to be blameless, kind, loving.

3. Wing-Tsit-Chan, quoting H. F. McNair in *The Way of Lao Tzu* (New York: Prentice Hall, 1963), 8.

Part IV

WAYS TO LIVE HAPPILY

11

THE MOST IMPORTANT THING IN LIFE

What is the most important thing in life? This is not a trick question. Think about it. How would you answer? When confronted with the question a group of students respond with things like love, happiness, peace of mind, good health, a good job. Wonderful answers, but not quite right. Many of us might answer from our personal condition. When asked what I wanted out of rehab, I said, "Peace of mind!" I can certainly identify with the student who offered that answer. I might also say to live without pain. I can't recall when I last woke not hurting somewhere. But we know such responses come from personal need and are thus somehow not *most* important. Isn't it interesting how quickly answers jump to abstract fulfillments, generally pleasurable?

No, the question is simpler, more basic. The answer is something you have done all your life, something you still do thousands of times a day without thinking. The most important thing in your life is your breath. Without it you die. It is wholly in the present. You can't breathe yesterday. You can't breathe tomorrow. You can only breathe right now. It is fundamental. There are no thoughts attached. You do not need to be taught its essential nature. You can't not breathe. As kids we used to hyperventilate and then hold our breaths to see who would pass out first. Someone always did, and when they did they started breathing again immediately. If you don't think it's basic, have someone come up behind you and clamp a large hand over your mouth and nose so you can't breathe. What is your reaction . . . even thinking about it? You don't have to have to use much imagination to figure that one out.

My cousin, who has become deeply involved in Tibetan-style Buddhist practice, told me recently he was going to visit a Bön Tantric master: "It's amazing. He lives the Dharma every moment, every day, even in his sleep!" "Tony," I said, "you have no choice." The act of breathing is living the Dharma. You cannot *not* do it and be. This is why it is central to the core practice of Zen Buddhism—meditation, zazen. Breathing is where zazen begins. Zazen is where Zen practice begins, if one could say such a thing has any real beginning. What could be simpler?

Many books have been written about zazen and Zen practice by certified Zen masters. I am not such a master and cannot presume to add anything to their teachings. My experience as volunteer chaplain at the university and as meditation chaplain at Tully Hill Treatment Center, a progressive drug and alcohol rehab facility, has been to give very basic instruction and to answer common questions that nearly everyone seems to bring to their first encounters with meditation. But since I have been blathering on about the centrality of zazen to Zen practice and by extension to living the life of St. Nadie—the life of no-one-ness—perhaps a brief, practical introduction might help anyone not familiar with the books and teachings to which I alluded above.

What is meditation?

Meditation helps us live in the present rather than being stuck in the past or anxious about the future. It helps bring clarity and compassion to our relationships with anything and to the events of our life. It is a simple, powerful means of achieving serenity. Most people have heard of it, but there are many misconceptions. It is a simple technique for calming the body and mind by staying in the present. Meditation is not magic. You just do it. It is done in silence and involves focusing and quieting the mind. One of the oldest, simplest, and best meditation practices is following your breath.

Is it different from contemplation?

Contemplation is a form of meditation that engages the mind on a particular subject or question, often a spiritual one. Anyone can meditate, but it *is* a practice. That is, with practice and with time, it deepens.

Do I have to believe in anything particular to make it work?

No. Meditation is a tool, not a belief system. People of all faiths and of no faith can and do practice meditation. Once, at Tully Hill, I was confronted by a biker in the teaching room. He hadn't been there very long. This was before we were able to convince the staff that first-weekers had not yet detoxed enough to participate. His tattooed arms bulged out of his sleeveless denim shirt. He was the only one not wearing sneakers, but heavy black boots instead. His very long ponytail was bound with an old rubber band. He pushed his face into mine.

"I don't believe in any of this fucking bullshit!"

"You don't have to believe in anything," I told him calmly, though a bit shaken. He was a little taken aback that I stood up to him. "I can't force you to do anything. All I ask is that you respect the right of others here to learn what I have to teach them. Just sit still and keep quiet."

He did that. In the end he even tried it out.

A Catholic nun, Sister Jeanine, sat with me a few times at Dai Bosatsu monastery. She said that, to her, zazen was a form of prayer. She saw no conflict with her deeply held beliefs or her vocation.

"Silence is the deepest prayer you can speak," she said.

Is there any danger in practicing meditation?

It is as safe as sitting in a chair or on a meditation cushion. Giving the body and mind, especially the autonomic nervous system, deep rest can have powerful healing effects. As the practice matures, however, it helps to have an experienced teacher or guide. Our minds are subtle and complex and it is necessary to have someone who has been through the experience help you understand the things that can go on in your mind that are confusing, sometimes even frightening or wildly pleasurable.

Someone who had been in recovery a year or so came to me expressing concern over what he called "blanks." He was experiencing something very like a blackout. It reminded him of his drinking days when he would have these periods of activity of which he would have no recollection at all. I had experienced blackouts too. Not prolonged ones, usually for a few minutes and sometimes for maybe an hour. They are scary. You haven't a clue what you've been doing. Yet here you are finishing something you can't recall starting, or standing in a room you can't recall entering, or driving someplace when you can't even recall getting in the car, much less where you're going. I understood his concern. What he was experiencing in meditation was a different phenomenon, though it may have felt the same. When you no longer pay attention to your thoughts you may find, even though you have had plenty of thoughts, that you don't remember them very well, that they aren't as substantive as they once seemed, that your mind is a bit "blank." The anxiety passes, as does the forgetfulness. He was relieved that he wasn't having some sort of relapse, but he wouldn't have known without a guide.

How will I know it is working?

Everybody expects something. It is important to remember it is not the same every time. You may experience calmness one day and anxiety the next. It doesn't really matter. What matters is that you do it. The effects of meditation are subtle and show up over time. It is not a quick fix. You will be calmer (overall), more alert, more open, less reactive and angry, more at peace. You will know it is working when someone tells you how you've changed, how you seem to smile more. As for what you get in return for sitting still and following your breath? Well, you will discover what is already there—a calm center rooted in the present, enabling you to respond to the world appropriately rather than reacting inappropriately. A clearer mind allows helpful choice to emerge. A calmer self allows you to risk opening yourself to others. Being open does not mean being vulnerable. Being vulnerable means you have something fragile (like your ego) to protect. Being open means your heart is like an open window that lets the winds of the world blow through without judgment or fear.

When should I meditate and for how long?

Traditionally, the ideal times to sit in meditation are dawn and dusk. That is almost impossible for most people these days. Once a day is enough, but twice is better. Just after you wake up, after you pee and wash your face but before you eat breakfast, is the most common time, and it helps you prepare for the day ahead. You can also do it in the evening, perhaps an hour or so before you would typically go to bed. Practicing too close to bedtime may cause you to wake up energized from the meditation when you actually need the sleep.

In the beginning, I think it is important to keep it simple. Begin with sitting periods of ten or fifteen minutes. I have found that beginners are enthusiastic and will determinedly plunk down for thirty minutes or an hour. After a week or so something may come up, an early meeting or a holiday, which makes it hard to sit for that long. So they don't. Then a little later it's something else and it gets easier and easier not to sit. Soon it is impossible to find an hour or even thirty minutes of free time, and they stop sitting altogether. I have found that if you keep it short it is easier to keep it consistent. After a month or two you will discover that, like skipping a meal, if you miss a sitting a part of you is missing too. You can't wait to get back to the routine. You will be hungry for it. That is a good time to add another five or ten minutes to your sitting periods. You can continue in this way, adding five minutes or so each month until you are up to thirty or forty minutes. If you force it, if you force anything in the practice, you easily become discouraged and find reasons not to practice. You can push yourself and the practice at intensive retreats, but until it is a living part of you, be kind to yourself and nurture the practice.

Suppose I think it isn't "doing" anything for me, that it's a dead loss?

We all have expectations even though the teachings admonish us not to. I first got seriously interested in meditation when I saw what it did for a friend. He was a dancer and a very hyper sort of guy. "Intense" barely touches it. He studied Transcendental Meditation, or TM, which was very big back when we were young. I saw him transformed from someone always anxious and confused into someone centered and calm, someone who smiled a lot. I thought, hmm, I'd like some of that.

Those were my expectations when I first began sitting. Meditation is not medicine. There is no peace-of-mind pill or enlightenment shot. It is a tool, a method. You have to use it to make it work. You may not notice anything at all in the beginning. You may even feel, like that biker, that you don't need or want it. Yet you will find its benefits accumulating and paying off when you least expect. One fellow at Tully Hill told me he didn't like the quiet. He liked having people around talking, the radio on, stuff happening. He didn't like listening to himself. Some time later I heard from him. He said that for some reason he'd kept it up, that one of his counselors had told him that in order to recover he needed to start listening to himself to heal himself. He did it even though he didn't like it. Now, with tears flowing freely, he told me he had, for the first time he could remember in his life, tasted a little peace. "For peace comes dropping slow, dropping from the veils of the morning . . ." as Yeats says.

Here is some of my basic instruction. There are many traditions of meditation, ancient and modern, all aimed at focusing and quieting the mind. The technique is less important, frankly, than the actual doing itself. If you practice this method of silently following your breath:

- be patient
- let it happen
- keep it simple

Do not complicate it with expectations or artificial goals. They already clutter too much of our lives. It is not a task or a job. It is a precious opportunity to discover yourself and, in the process of discovery, to open up to the being we all share in common.

There are two parts to the instruction: (1) posture and (2) technique.

Posture

The idea is to create a stable, balanced posture. You can sit on a cushion, kneel with a bench or some other support, or use a chair. There are no demerits for using a chair, just a few extra considerations.

- On a *zafu*, or any sitting cushion, sit cross-legged in a way that allows both knees to touch the floor or mat. You are creating a tripod between your tail bone and knees. This provides a low center of gravity that is stable. With practice, one can hold it a long time.
- Sit forward on the edge of the cushion.
- Many people in the West find it hard to sit in the full lotus posture with ankles up on each thigh. Do not force yourself. Manage what you can without cutting off your circulation.
- Keep your spine erect. This is easier sitting cross-legged. You have to be more conscious of keeping it that way when you kneel or use a chair.

- Shoulders are relaxed. Imagine that your body is suspended from a piece of string attached to the top of your head and that you are simply hanging loose and straight. If you are kneeling, using the *seiza* posture, keep the same things in mind.
- If you are sitting in a chair, sit straight, keeping the feet flat on the floor.

  When you bend your back or let it sag you tend to daydream more and become drowsy. By thinking of the tension in your body slowly flowing out of it into the floor, release the tension in your jaw, face, neck, shoulders, arms, hands, abdomen, and legs.

  Your abdomen should be relaxed. There is no need for washboard abs in zazen.
- Rest your hands in your lap, grasping your left thumb with your right hand and then gently embracing your right hand with your left, forming a loose fist. You can also rest the back of the left hand on the palm of the right and let your thumbs touch, forming a circle. These hand positions are called *mudra* and help direct the form of the energy your body generates.
- Keep your eyes open but lower the lids a little, gazing at the floor in front of you. The intention is to be awake, alert, aware, *present*. With your eyes closed you daydream and doze.

Technique

- Now, inhale and exhale through your nose (unless you have a cold). Do not force your breath to be deep or slow, nor should you speed it up. Just allow yourself to breathe naturally, easily. It will slow and deepen of its own accord as you settle into meditation.
- Feel, even listen to the breath as it leaves and enters your nostrils, moves gently into your lungs and out again.
- Pay attention just to your breath. Discover your own rhythm.
- Begin following the up and down motion of the breathing in your abdomen and chest. Feel its flow and texture.

- When you have begun to sense your own rhythm, the flow of your own breath, begin counting the breaths. Silently in your mind with each exhalation, the whole length of that out breath, count *one*. Hold the silent sound of *one* throughout the entire exhalation. Follow with *twwooo . . .* immediately on the next exhalation, and so on.
- Continue until you reach *ten* then return to one.

That's all there is to it. Except you probably will never get to ten. At maybe four your mind starts to wander. Carefully inhabit each breath. Each and every time your mind wanders, for whatever reason (an itch, a noise, hunger, a sore knee . . . it will wander often) return and begin again at one.

There is a common misconception that in meditation you are supposed to make your mind go blank. It is the nature of your mind to think. When you try to force the mind not to do what is in its nature, you engage it and create dualities that further tangle it. As you pay less attention to the noise in your head, the mind begins to calm and the noise to subside into a murmur. The mind becomes less active.

So return and begin at *one* as often as you find yourself caught up in thought and away from the breath. Neither judge nor criticize yourself; just return to the breath. You have the rest of the day to reminisce, worry, plan. Now is the time to be quiet. Allow thoughts to come and go like clouds in the sky or leaves in a stream. Do not deny them, but neither should you engage them.

"There goes a red leaf, there's a yellow one."

"There goes an angry thought."

What normally happens? We think, "That bastard really pissed me off. If I see him again . . ." and we're off someplace else with our anger, caught in the stream, pulled away from the moment. Likewise, if we say, "Oh, I'm not supposed to be angry. That's a bad feeling. I'm supposed to be calm and meditate," we are reacting to and engaging the anger by denying it. Accept that bit of anger. "Yup, I'm really angry when I think of what he said." Then go back to your breath. You may have to do this several times!

The same applies to a pleasant thought. "That was so much fun last night. I hope I get to see him again . . ." and we're gone off into some blissful daydream away from here and now. Don't fight it. Acknowledge the pleasure, the joy. Then go back to your breath. In reality all these things pass anyway. Let them pass in thought as well. *This* is your life. Taste it now.

Despite our longing to ease our souls, we will question anyone offering anything that sounds like a solution. I think this is a good thing. Answers to the big questions have been to many people the great "no-shows," as Charles Simic calls them. This attitude can be very annoying to teachers, especially Asian teachers, accustomed to respect and obedience. But doubt is helpful. It should not, however, be confused with frustrated expectations. "So what?" is very different from "What's in it for me?" One of the "values" of breath awareness is that it requires no articles of faith. You don't have to believe in your breathing, you just do it.

KNOW THAT AFTER ALL
LIFE IS SIMPLE
DO NOT COMPLICATE IT

This morning at breakfast
as we touch our teacups together
and listen to the news
tell me your name again
for I always forget.

Zazen is transforming. It is the agent for change both large and small. In AA they say that if you were a drunken asshole and then you sober up, you become a sober asshole. Being sober does not relieve you of the responsibility of working on your assholeness. Likewise, one may have some sort of insight experience and remain a fool. Zazen compels one to face one's foolishness and deal with it.

And it really is a practice. You have to keep at it. Doing zazen does not confer any honors or rights. It is more like going to the gym. When you first go, you're out of shape and everything is difficult. After a few weeks what was difficult initially becomes easy and you move on to more challenging things. But if you stop, you get out of shape again and you slide back to where you were. You simply have to keep at it. Further, you don't go to the gym merely to see how much you can bench-press or how fast you can run. You do these things so that when you are in the world—at work, on a hiking or canoe trip, anything that demands use of your body—your heart and muscles are in a condition to cope, to make your experience of those activities more engaged and complete, less concerned with what you can't do and more with what you can. You likewise sit in zazen so that when you are in the world you are more clear-headed, open-hearted, energized to take on the anomalies of life with equanimity.

A student once said to me that he did his meditation in the woods, at the beach watching a sunset, or sitting on a mountain. How much richer, I suggested, those moments would be if he were "in shape" spiritually through a strong meditative practice. The peaceful silence of the woods enriched by his own deeper awareness, the sound of the waves taking him out of himself clearly and completely.

For me, the appeal of Zen has always been its simplicity and directness. It is not interested in power or control. Zen has its esoteric aspects. They have always seemed secondary to me, like the shamanistic cults in Tibetan practice—means of controlling and defining things that are not central, essential. Very likely I have this wrong. But where I see power and control I see traps, traps that take me away from my essential work.

When Myo-On Maurine Stuart was interviewing me for the *Jukai* (Precepts) ceremony, she asked me, "What is your work?" We got into a discussion of my day job as a librarian versus my vocation as a poet and a father. Now I would answer, "Zazen is my work!" In the Tao Te Ching we read:

> We work with being
> but non-being is what we use.

And thus, the work, the practice, must be endless.

12

GIVING UP GIVING UP

Anything I write is not Zen. It is about Zen, and maybe not even that. James Austin, in his fascinating book of neurophysiology *Zen and the Brain*, cites eight things about Zen that seem to me true, as far as they go, and perhaps point to a way of understanding the experience of Zen.

The first is, as I have already noted, that meditation is central to Zen practice. It is the way to awakening, to understanding without conditions that we and the universe are coexistent, that we are indeed derived from stardust, that we can experience this interconnectedness and in experiencing it realize there is nothing to add, that everything is all right here now.

The second point is that intellect is not at home in Zen. Those who know do not speak. "The Tao that can be told is not the true Tao." So why does everyone, including myself, keep going on about it?

Thirdly, Zen, not unlike science, values simple, concrete, living facts of everyday direct personal experience (observation is only part of what we experience), to perceive "livingly" without analysis. This just drives people nuts. There has to be something to figure out, a puzzle to solve. How can we understand without reasoning why? How can we trust the authenticity of experience when we cannot share it with another? Isn't reason and analysis our way of sharing? Only sometimes. When I am in love (and even logicians fall in love) I know and she knows and neither of us has to analyze anything.

Zen is, fourthly and perhaps most importantly, intensely pragmatic, wary of moral judgments. As Austin puts it:

> Its security comes from knowing, as a result of long experience, how people act after they have become totally committed to it. . . . Why burden them with another superstructure of someone else's doctrines imposed from without? Their behavior is going to become increasingly selfless anyway, because it will be proceeding in harmony with the natural order of things.

A woman once became bitterly angry with me because I made some statement regarding the conditional nature of good and evil. She insisted that evil exists independently and that we need to know it to fight it. Experience has taught me differently. She needed a "real" evil to feed her anger, an anger some might say was justified perhaps because of brutality she experienced in her past. Somewhere the cycle that breeds violence and anger must be broken. The breaking comes in our taking responsibility for our responses to it and for our actions, learning over time what appropriate action means. The practice of zazen leads one there. And this is Austin's fifth point: you learn about Zen in zazen. Also, he adds in his next point, the sixth, you needn't sit on a cushion to practice Zen. Zen is, he says, "paying bare attention to all events of daily life"—learning to be goal-less and selfless slowly, like the process of evolution.

If, as he says in his seventh point, Zen stresses self-reliance, self-discipline, and personal effort, why do we need a teacher? A teacher cannot make you experience anything. A good teacher is a mirror. When you go to *dokusan* (a private, formal interview with your teacher) it is not to engage your teacher but to meet yourself—as you truly are in the world, all fantasies and deprecations aside. You get to see what you have been avoiding about yourself, which of course makes one anxious as you anticipate it. My teachers, Eido Roshi and Shinge Roshi, are particularly adept in teaching this way: if you need a shove, they give it; if you need a gentle voice of encouragement, they give it; if you are a fool, they let you see it; if you understand, they acknowledge it; if you need a kick in the butt, you'll get it. A teacher has been there. They have been there with their own ego-battles, their own suffering. What you bring them is familiar ground. It has been said that a teacher can tell your condition by the sound of your footsteps approaching the room. I have spent hours sitting sesshin, concocting something to tell the teacher, convincing myself it is a true expression of the Dharma. It is, of course, but not in the way I would like to think. Secretly, even unknown to myself, I want it to be *my* expression.

When I enter the dokusan room, the hours of convoluted reasoning fly away and I have nothing to say. Have I made a fool of myself? Only to myself. A teacher can make that clear by just being there. Not pointing a finger or blaming you for getting it wrong, but by being a selfless expression of the Dharma before your eyes. You see your own vanity in their clear, shining reflection of who you are. I have no clue how this is done, but I do know it is essential. It is a constantly refreshing return to the truth. In the Rinzai tradition a teacher keeps you aware of the urgency of the practice: that you have only this life, this day, this moment to wake up. Why wait?

The Tisarana are three vows one takes with the Precepts and which we recite with each morning service, sometimes called the Three Refuges. The usual translation is:

> I take refuge in the Buddha.
> I take refuge in the Dharma.
> I take refuge in the Sangha.

Eido Roshi feels that this translation does not capture the spirit of the practice. It should be:

I give my life to the Buddha.
I give my life to the Dharma.
I give my life to the Sangha.

To many this may have the scent of self-flagellation. I'll give up everything and then I'll finally get it. No. You have also to give up giving up. And you can't wait around for tomorrow.

A good friend and spiritual guardian (my sponsor when I was ordained) once told me that in dokusan he came in, made his bows, and said to Roshi, "Just sitting!" He felt he had really gotten that expression, used so often in Roshi's own talks, that he had penetrated it and absorbed its essence. He spoke it, he thought, with the right emphasis for Roshi to see how clear his understanding was. Roshi smiled. He leaned over and drew a line on the floor with his finger in front of my friend's knees. "Sit as though this were the edge of the universe!"

Austin's eighth point is the issue of the *bodhisattva* (what we might call an awake awakening being), of what we do with ourselves outside of meditation. The inner journey is but a prelude to going out, like twelfth-step work, taking one's experience to others with a helping hand. It is anything but a denial of the world or a negative withdrawal into isolation, something the West has accused Buddhism of for centuries. For it is not *what* happens to you, but *how* you carry it into life each day, moment by moment, so that others may also wake up. Awareness is helping each of us sense what we need to know; that perhaps it is not death we fear, but rather *not living*—which is altogether different.

Admiral Richard E. Byrd wrote in the introductory pages of his book, *Alone*, about a solo winter in the Antarctic, during which he faced death and insanity moment by moment:

And it is surprising, approaching the final enlightenment, how little one really has to know or feel sure about.

There is always a point in conversations about Zen and Buddhism when someone asks about *karma*. Karma is simply the law of cause and effect extended to all things and all acts in all times—not just to physical matter. To us in the West it sounds a lot like fatalism. "It's his karma to have cancer" or "That guy has good karma. He has all the luck." No, that's like saying karma and luck are the same. It is also like saying "God told me to." Or "The devil made me do it." This approach tries to erase responsibility, which karma does not. What I understand, if you could call it understanding at all, is that there is only one event and it is taking place all the time. Abbot of the Nebraska Zen Center, Nonin Chowaney, writes:

> How we handle present conditions determines subsequent conditions. What we are now determines what we will be. . . . This does not mean passivity. . . . This doesn't mean we have to like our circumstances or not take any steps to cure them. When dealing with our circumstances, or when facing injustice, violence, or social and economic imbalance, we need to act and encourage others to act in ways that alleviate our own suffering and that of all beings.

When confronted by the overwhelming suffering in the world, we grab our egos tightly. "Well, Bosnia, yeah, but that's not my karma." "Oh, I could never be Mother Teresa." "Not everyone can be Albert Schweitzer and go trapsing off into the jungle. That was *his* karma. Someone has to make the cars, the medical supplies, grow the food!" "How could I make a difference anyway?"

Listen to the *Parable of the Starfish*:

> Once there was a terrible storm at sea. It raged all night, heaving huge waves up along the coast, battering everything along the shore. Tides were many feet above normal. No one could recall such a violent storm in years.

In the morning all was calm again, but the beaches were a mess; in many places they had been washed away altogether and sections of cliff had collapsed. Along other stretches wrecks of boats, timber, trash, and seawrack cluttered the dunes and salt grass. For miles along one stretch of shore, thousands upon thousands of starfish had been washed up above the tide line.

An old man wandered up the littered beach, occasionally poking at a dead starfish among the many. He shook his head. He didn't think starfish particularly valuable. He didn't think much of them at all. But so much death. What a waste. Who'd have thought there could be so many starfish just on this bit of beach alone? He shook his head again, feeling helpless.

At one point he looked up and saw a small figure moving toward him. It was moving slowly, perhaps a child or a small woman, stopping occasionally to throw something into the sea. Eventually they met up. It was indeed a child, a boy, and he was stooping among the dead starfish, then throwing some into the sea.

"Good morning, son, what are you up to?" the old man asked.

"I'm looking for starfish that are still alive and throwing them back into the ocean so they can stay that way."

The old man looked up and down the long beach, at the thousands of dead and dying starfish.

"That's very nice, son, but what difference could you possibly make in all this?"

The boy looked at the slowly moving starfish in his hand. "Well, sir, it sure makes a difference to *this* one!" and he tossed it into the waves.

Be Positive under Any Circumstances

Let me say that I love you
when you lie ringed with death.
Though love cannot always find a way
out of your fear,
it is not for your life
but for your truth you are afraid.
The blessing is not that we say you are true
but that you are.

One of my favorite painters is Helen Frankenthaler. She is a lucid witness of color as compassion—selfless clarity beyond abstraction. For Frankenthaler, as I see her work, abstraction is like a song rising from color and shape to speak truth without conditions. The full impact of her work struck me at an exhibition of her prints in the National Gallery. I had been at conferences for nearly three weeks. I was beat up and meeting-ed out. The last one was in Washington and I had a few hours to kill before my flight home. I had no idea what was showing and just wandered in looking for some private time.

Coming upon the Frankenthaler show was like entering a church. Even with crowds milling about there was a deeper silence in her fluid abstractions that said "this is something holy, this is true." The pinnacle for me was a modest piece called "Sun After Rain," a glowing vibrant blue and yellow print that made me catch my breath, made my eyes tear up, much as the actual sun flashing out after rain might do. From her show I drifted up some stairs to discover another show of David Smith sculptures arranged in an amphitheater manner. I was surrounded by strange beings that had the palpable shape of all my selves and all my demons, as though they were gathered to meet and pray with me, or to burst into some Greek chorus of fluid nameless chant. I staggered back to the Frankenthaler, past a brilliant metallic screen, and back outside. I had been given a gift and I still do not know what the gift is or means save only that I live more and better because of it. It is what art does.

At one time she was married to Robert Motherwell, whose work I like almost as much. He wrote in this context—of the meaning of art—often. Motherwell wrote movingly on many things, including Kafka. He could have written it about the intensity of our practice. Regarding Kafka, he wrote:

> To read him is to be marked for life . . . marked by the reality
> of inwardness, that most sacred of modern domains of which
> he is a vivid witness. The more subjective and the more faith-

ful to one's own truth that one becomes, the more objective one becomes as a witness to historical truth.

This objectivity can be seen in what I call "The Mirror of St. Nadie." What is it? A rain puddle.

There is another parable, this one about a Rabbi:

> A man came to the Rabbi and said, "Rabbi, it is written that once we could see the face of God. Why can't we do that anymore? What happened that men can no longer reach that high to see the face of God?"
>
> The rabbi was very old. He had seen it all. He closed his eyes and ran his fingers through his long beard.
>
> "My son, that is not it at all. Men cannot see the face of God because no one can stoop that low."

When I was seventeen I won the school discus cup for my house at school in England. I did it by pure will, out-distancing better, stronger boys, an act of pure determination without grace or skill. This minor victory reflects the way I have distrusted the truth of myself throughout my life.

A few weeks prior to the track and field affair in which I won the cup, I was on the practice fields doing endless repetitions of the quick, graceful (sometimes), spinning dance one uses to hurl the discus. My coach, a retired Olympic weight lifter from Scotland, had great hopes for me. He felt I had decathlon potential. It really amounted to my being second or third best in most events without excelling in any (most kids specialized in sprints or distance or *something*). I was one of the last on the fields this particular afternoon. Tired, too tired to think about the steps, the grip, the need to put my body's energy behind the whirl of my arm and not use more than mere arm strength to throw the weighted wood and metal disc. I could never get this last part right.

My arms were simply not strong enough to do it alone and I typically came in third or fourth against boys whose technique was better. I stood there, looking up from the divots the discus had left in the grass, over the towers of the school to the Channel beyond the town of Ramsgate, just able to pick out the white cliffs of France some thirty miles away.

"Once more," I thought. I needed a shower and food! My fingers folded over the metal edge. My palm felt flat against the metal core. The wood between was rough on this practice discus, used for who knows how many generations of English boys. I turned away, closed my eyes, took a breath, turned my left foot out as I prepared to spin on it, and began to swing my extended right arm behind me. Then I unleashed into the two turns like a spring. The discus left my hand as I bounced on my right foot. I watched it go. When it reached my best mark of the day it hadn't yet peaked in the extraordinary arc it was taking. It kept going, further than anything I had done before, further than any boy in the school could have dreamed of throwing it.

I was stunned. What had I done? How did I do it? There was no one else around to witness it. Wow! I have to do that again, I thought. I couldn't know that "I" hadn't done anything, that "I" hadn't been there at all, that the throw did the throwing. After an hour of fruitless, exhausted attempts to duplicate it, I gave up and went in.

Knowing I had done it and not knowing how, I was determined by pure will to prove I could do it before the whole school. The winning throw was far short of what I had done that evening alone, all arm again. John Savage, my closest competitor, was tired and out of form, having just edged me in the quarter-mile. So I beat him. I look back on that victory with shame.

Humbly Obey the Law of the Universe

Looking up, cold spring rains
splatter over my face
and run under my collar.
Looking down, the drops splatter
into the puddle at my feet.
That tall reflection of someone
vanishes.

The Tao Te Ching says:

> When the Tao (or Way) is lost, there is goodness,
> When goodness is lost, there is morality,
> When morality is lost, there is ritual.
> Ritual is the husk of faith,
> The beginning of chaos.

I wanted (Eden's sin) the truth of what I thought I could do to be seen by all. A good athlete trusts his body and does not rely on the lesser strength of his will. I did not know that. I could no longer sense, either, that I no longer trusted my own truth in the universe, that by ignoring the voice of St. Nadie and not disappearing into everything, I had become a husk, willful and hard, ripe for failure, a player in the ritual of being rather than the humble, anonymous actuality of being.

Part V

A BOY RUNNING IN THE WIND

13

THE MERCIFUL AVATAR

We can be so humorless about joy. This has always struck me as very peculiar. One can get this impression of seriousness from the solemn atmosphere of churches in which one finds oneself speaking in hushed tones, or from the motionless silence of the zendo. People with heads bowed, all these folks lined up working at keeping their traps shut, waiting for the light of joy. In Buddhism there is the phenomenon of the *merciful avatar*. Commonly, the merciful avatar is understood to be a manifestation of the Buddha sent to teach you not to be such an egotistical jerk. It can be a bird, as in Issa's wonderful poem:

> Flying out from
> the great Buddha's nose
> a swallow.

When someone cuts you off while driving—the merciful avatar at work. When someone at a meeting humiliates you with a cutting remark—the merciful avatar just doing his job. It assumes other manifestations, such as when you are feeling a bit superior or that you have got some sort of clue into what is going on.

There was once a chap at Dai Bosatsu monastery who could not sit still in the zendo, who could not even keep his *rakasu*, a vestment worn over the robe, straight. He dropped jellybeans during *kinhin*, walking meditation. He took too much tea and then spilled it on himself, his cushion, and the floor in front of him. He looked more like a drunken Friar Tuck than an austere Buddhist ascetic. He was a mess. He made everyone feel great.

Each of us did so much better, were so obviously superior, that we tolerated, nay welcomed, his insufficiencies as a contrast to our own. Then, one day, on a warm, very still afternoon, when the silence of the zendo was deepest, when even he seemed to be silent and still, and samadhi seemed at hand for everyone, he leaned slightly to one side and farted.

Hugely, freely, Dharma thunder.

Everyone's serenity vanished instantly in snickers, giggles, and eventual roars of laughter. Until the jikijitsu had to bellow for everyone to be still. Each of us groaned in the agony of keeping laughter in. No thought was given to the True Way. He shattered our holy fantasies. The usual distinction between men and women, that the former find farts funny and the latter do not, was lost and meaningless. I wrote a tribute to this merciful avatar with lines drawn from so-called sacred texts.

A Merciful Avatar Farts in the Zendo

This truth,
incomparably profound and minutely subtle,
is hardly met with
even in hundreds of thousands of millions of eons.
No thought, no volition,
no consciousness, no suffering.
If we listen to this truth
and praise it
and gladly embrace it
we have really gone beyond foolish talk.
We now can see this,
listen to this,
accept and hold this.
As the truth eternally reveals itself
at this moment
what more need we seek?
How transparent the perfect moonlight.
How boundless the cleared sky.
The gate of oneness
of cause and effect is opened.

You have the right to remain miserable. Any joy you express will certainly be used against you. Smile, you're on camera. We don't want to know how you really feel, but we are sure it is bad. One of the comical ironies of our world (at least it would be comical if it weren't so pathetic) is that we offer ready access to the ten thousand pleasures but we cannot enjoy them unless we recognize they are wrong on some level and that unhappiness is our proper state.

You think I am kidding? Ask someone how they are. Most people say they are fine. Of course, we know they are being polite. So we probe a little. We wonder what they're hiding. If we're lucky, a pointed question or two will unleash a flood of bitterness or anger. If someone replies to our question that they are doing poorly, we unquestioningly validate his or her suffering, grief, or anger, but we almost always question pleasure or, dread word, joy. What have you got to smile about? Life's a bitch, then you die. Only a country weaned on the Puritan work ethic would have that as a bumper sticker.

For years I have wondered about this. Why can't we embrace someone who can say, in all honesty, "I'm great; life is wonderful"? Some years ago, John Updike wrote in the *New York Review of Books*, "Puritanism (in its world-hating heart) admires, as the ultimate proof of sincerity, self-destruction. . . ." He was talking about the veritable cult the U.S. has in the arts—from painting and poetry to rock-and-roll—of young artists flaming up joyously and then destroying themselves. Clearly at some level as a culture we hate ourselves, hate life, and celebrate those who tell us we are wrong. We are afraid. We admire and fear the courage of brave men or women as stalked by fear as we are.

Some years ago there was an anti-substance-abuse ad in our campus paper showing a photo of a young girl on her knees draped over a toilet. The caption read, "Are we having fun yet?" Perhaps, as a drinker, this ad had special poignancy for me. It also told me something is really wrong. In Al Anon they teach "the three C's." These were important tools for my wife's recovery from my alcoholism. They also go a long way toward helping us face and cope with what can seem like the unrelenting misery of the world. They are: you did not **C**ause it; you cannot **C**ure it; and you cannot **C**ontrol it.

They allowed my wife to detach from my addiction and allowed me to take responsibility for my own behavior. But they leave out one piece that would make them complete. It was something I came to understand a very little as I studied the koan "Hyakujo's Fox" (which I did not understand well at all). In that koan a teacher is compelled to be reborn as a fox for five hundred lifetimes for telling a student that an enlightened man is not affected by the laws of cause and effect, or karma. Hyakujo told the man/fox that the enlightened man cannot *ignore* the laws of cause and effect.

We may not cause, cure, or control someone's addiction, or other misery they may have, but we cannot ignore it either. We are each thing always, all the time. The universe is not a burden. A burden suggests there is something separate from ourselves to carry. There is not. We are the expression of the universe, the voice of the Dharma, and to ignore anything in it divides us from all of it.

14

WILD APPLES, CROWS IN THE RAIN

But of course each of us does carry a burden. For some of us the burdens are so huge we simply collapse, or we create a script of bitterness that we recite regularly to anyone who will listen. We know it will be more readily validated than any joy we might have experienced. In my recovery I had created my own script:

"Writing is my life.

"I have to drink in order to write.

"I have to drink so much in order to write that I can't write.

"Drink is killing me, literally."

Before I went into rehab and for a long time after, I recited this script in several well-rehearsed versions to affirm my own misery, to explain away why I could no longer do what had been at the core of my life for thirty years, to listen to myself as though that made me real, made my inability to write real and somehow valid.

Then one night I had a dream. It was a prescient dream, I think. I do not normally give too much credence to dreams beyond their being a working out of some subconscious issues and the day's events. I do not attach meaning to so-called symbols, nor do I see anything mystical in them. But this one stands before me stronger than my memory of today's breakfast. I should add, perhaps, that this dream was an exaggerated version of earlier ones in which I found myself having to encounter a person with his or her back turned, ordinary seeming enough, whom I somehow knew to be death. Usually the person was dressed like a postman. If I saw the face I would die. I always woke up just as the person turned around.

In the usual inexplicable way of "facts" in dreams, the fact was that the street in front of our house was lined with hospital beds, much like parked cars. Each one had a napping child in it, watched over by a parent. I was out there with the others, my son in the bed. The canopy of trees arching over the street was greater in the dream than in reality, forming a green tunnel to the main street, a couple of houses away, but otherwise everything was as usual. All of the parents standing by the beds were staring toward the end of the tree tunnel. We were hearing terrible screams.

Then we saw a man run by as fast as humanly possible, screaming in total terror. Seconds later he was followed by a large (maybe eight-foot-tall), one-legged, demon-like creature with huge muscular arms and a large mouth. We could each see these things because the creature paused in his one-legged bounding and looked up our street. We stood frozen in place. He then turned and caught up to the fleeing man and we heard his screams as he was torn limb from limb alive and then devoured. The screams ended and we were still paralyzed in our places. We knew it would return.

In a bound it appeared at the end of the street. Everyone just stared. In a leap it was on the first bed, just before the one my son was on. It swatted the parent aside like tissue, picked up the child by an ankle, and opened its startlingly wide mouth, looking at me out of the corner of its eye. I whipped up my hands and made a sign. It was a sign of power, something I knew evil feared. As I did I could feel my mouth working to say, to shout something, but nothing came out. The creature dropped the child, looking suddenly fearful, backed down the street and disappeared. Fear was its power and rule. I had overcome it. My wife woke me gently, saying I was groaning. I rose up, suddenly aware I was no longer afraid of death.

With this experience I turned to face my writer's block. Everyone has heard of writer's block. When I experienced it in brief forms over the years I did not worry over much. I got, perhaps, a little depressed, a little anxious, but that was all. It seemed like the weather, a dry spell. But the rains would come again. They always did.

But after I left rehab I had had a two-year-plus stretch that was different. For the first time the rains seemed like they might never come again. It was more complicated than before, mixed up as it was with my drinking and attempts at recovery, my deepening Zen practice, my questioning in new ways who and what I was. What I thought I once knew no longer applied. It was scary. I may not have been very good as a poet but there was something about poetry that was so much a part of me that to give it up, to admit it was gone, was like saying I was dead.

Feeling like a zombie did not improve my chances for recovery and somehow this extended drought was not something I felt I could bring up at AA meetings, where there is a certain pressure to conform spiritually and culturally. It came, as always, back to me. The so-called joy of the oblivion of drink remained very appealing. I felt completely alone, unable to talk with anyone, loathing self-pity as much as loathing what I had done with my life. Ploddingly, I went to meetings. Hopelessly, I continued sitting. I began to see hope as an insidious thing, a tease, one of the seeds of bitterness. "Okay," I thought, "suppose I stop hoping?"

Then two things happened. These things were, again, curiously enough, art exhibitions. The Johnson Museum at Cornell University held a small but stunning exhibition called "The Art of Zen." A bunch of us from the Zen Center went down to see it, only seventy miles away. Here were the great classics of Zen art right in front of us. Icons of serenity and silence hung naked before us. Here were men—Fugai, Bankei, Obaku, Hakuin, Ryokan, Sengai—who stood in the absolute silence of eternity and remained silent, save for these few brush strokes. Across the centuries the prayer of silence spoke so loudly that my fears and self-pitying despair became very small and selfish. A crack appeared in my wall of oblivion. I saw the blind men of Hakuin on the log bridge and felt myself crawling helplessly with them. My mind leapt immediately to Bruegel's *The Parable of the Blind*, and my heart leapt with the familiar *Yes! Yes!*

About a month later I had to be in Washington for another conference. I went to the Hirshhorn in my spare time and chanced (or what I imagined was chance) upon a Francis Bacon exhibit. You cannot imagine anything more different from the serenity of Zen art than Francis Bacon. I was stunned. Suddenly the joyous silences of the Zen paintings rose up to meet the twisted screams of Bacon's butchered queens, bleeding popes—and they were the same, the silence and the scream. What was this? Something in me broke. My self-created walls of doubt and misery vanished before this total joy and total horror. How could these two seemingly opposite emotions and experiences be together? Both were at the heart of the human experience, utter joy as well as complete suffering.

Slowly I began to pull myself off the pity pot. Inexplicably, I was inspired to write a *renga*. A renga is, traditionally, a poem of one hundred linked verses, though the length can vary considerably, with stanzas of three and two lines, the last line of one verse becoming the first of the next. Traditionally, in Japan, a renga was created by two or more poets, playing off one another, in a kind of friendly competition over saké. I left the saké out of my equation, but in some ways the scream of Bacon's paintings and the silence of the Zen art became two voices. An incipient St. Nadie became the third. I called it "Wild Apples and Crows in the Rain." These seemed to represent the two art exhibitions I saw and some seeds in my own experience of life and death.

And so I began writing again.

The process of transformation was slow. Somehow my dream had given me the strength to break the wall of silence (and we are usually silent about the wall of death), had given me permission to take up a pen again. And write I did. In one rainy Sunday afternoon, in a blaze of unexpected energy, I wrote one hundred stanzas of two and three lines each. It lacks, overall, an essential music, but there are lines that still hold something true. In the end I cut what I wrote almost in half, but I literally wrote myself back into creative life, using the several voices of my confused being to open doors of joy, stealing lines from anything scribbled in my commonplace book, from Vita Sackville-West to book reviews, jumping and connecting every which way.

St. John and St. Theresa write about the dark night of the soul, the necessary abyss one must enter and from which one must emerge to express the joy that does not end. Experience tells me that we can know this abyss in many ways. Some are profound and life changing. Some are just bad days. Some people may encounter the profound dark only once, or not at all, others several times. Some find only that and pause forever. I think we know the levels of the abyss by degrees.

Perhaps, for me, working through this poem was somewhere between commonplace depression and suicidal despair, leaning a little more toward the latter. I was sure that if this did not work I was truly finished and that I might as well die. I might not kill myself, though I had been doing that all along with the drinking, but I would quit. But I was not a quitter! I had failed, but I was not a quitter! Perhaps I intuited the connection between the fear of failure and the fear of death, that ultimate failure by some perceptions. It was something I recognized I had inherited from my dad's family, an incredible stupidity about when to give up. But I had begun to think about this two-year wasteland, that if I didn't truly cross it this time, I would quit. It was a bitter secret I told no one.

Think how we reward power, no matter what it has done to whom. We admire the ruthless for their willingness to break the rules we think bind us. They make their own rules as we would like to but are unable to do. Yet we are victimized by what we admire. We will even reward the power of drugs and disease because they change the rules. Can we really take charge of our own lives?

Perhaps we have trouble with joy because we feel it has to be earned, while misery comes unbidden and undeserved. We earn joy by having the courage to accept the silence and the scream at once even while we fear them. I discovered that I do not deserve joy nor do I deserve misery. They are preferences. Part of this path that leads to something beyond joy is my slow uncovering of this now obvious seeming thing. "Wild Apples and Crows in the Rain" records that process.

That rainy afternoon, full of the raucous life of crows and the nostalgia of apples on the ground, the lines came unbidden, like drops of water running down the window, flowing together, choosing their own direction and meaning, building momentum as they flowed along. I wrote in a white heat, oblivious to the darkening room, the smells from the Sunday kitchen, the ache in my back. It is a cliché, but I wrote as if my life depended upon it—because it did.

I found myself recalling beggars in Spain, in the old city of La Laguna on Tenerife, "who sleep with hands outstretched, who wake with eyes like treeless wilds." I looked for the "unmoored meaning," but always a meaning, something in "the sleet of stars," in "laying the ash of grace." I paused paralyzed by the present. How do we face this poisoned present? How do we tell our children this broken place is their future?

Pat answers will not work. Work will work, but not purposeless effort for the sake of work itself, not for the *ethic* of work. The work that will work is the work of loving—loving even the flawed, the failed, even the hateful. Some people think there are rules for this. Some people need instruction about the right way to load toilet paper on the roller so they can wipe their asses clean correctly.

As I struggled with this poem, as I struggled with a self slowly losing its fear of failure, of death, I fought to understand this huge responsibility. Zen is famous for its freedom. Zen is famous for its discipline. Arguably a Rinzai monk or nun faces rigors more demanding than anything devised by the Jesuits. The Beats made what they thought was Zen freedom one of their hallmarks. But it was, at least in the early glory days before Ginsberg or Gary Snyder got serious about practice, an irresponsible freedom and so not really free at all. They wanted to be able to be crazy and free like Han Shan, the Cold Mountain poet. To be free you have to take responsibility for everything, no exceptions.

Finally the silence and the scream came together in me. The process of writing down the images that flooded through me tore at my denials, refusals, fears, disbeliefs, and desires—even the distinctions that some things could be noble, true, real.

A crow calls, the universe laughs.

An apple falls and the empire of our will trembles.

I realized I had become a memory of myself, as one does in the cycle of self-created fictions we generate, trying to get just one story believable enough, good enough for us to accept, to fit into whatever we wish reality to be. Bacon's faceless mouths or bodiless limbs or limbless bodies were my broken fictions, were everyone's broken fictions. The simple lines depicting large-eyed Daruma sitting, his back to my yearning, Kanzan laughing, really utterly free, the absolute *enso* (Zen circles) hanging in silence were my own and the universe's vast emptiness, nothing holy therein (they end only where they meet).

WILD APPLES, CROWS IN THE RAIN
(a *dokugin renga*)

we do not begin, we resume
in this shifting munching dark
one is silent the other screams
      daylight drags the dark pieces
      out of sight to the one place
thwarted by dusk
born late in a lump of head
bound to the senses
      that go on for a lifetime
      a tousled pilgrim mind
left by the door
with other shapes of hearsay
who sleep with hands outstretched
      who wake with eyes like treeless wilds
      who begot the cradled self
in the self abyss
the stranger from unhaunted magnitude
a hard gait on wet stone
      foxgrapes bracken scarfed in swathes of rain
      ravelled through the sunless days
the small tragedies of dark
overcome by inward grace
and the strength to be alone
      above the hedge with earth and sky
      where wing heaving black birds fly

how cold the fields under the verb of wind
wild apples scatter sweeten the ground
how long the silence of their throats
       strewing the days like bread broken into years
       laying down the song of autumn
cries of boys running careless as dusk
crows wheel and clack settle in some yard
releasing present out of some slow future
       you can hear the young ones cry
       from the nest in each hollow eye
greylunged against its going down
the dust of the sun
wet wanhopes wandering away
       among abandoned retreads by a road
       accumulated beginnings
messengers of nothing
but vacant nows
reasty apples grudge into earth
       gospel gaunt towns
       along dead railroads and dying rivers
feckless orphans in the cold
bones dangling from gloves
the failures of need
       the past and the future are ghost territories
       there is not then what is not now
a traceless beginning
cannot be lost
with nowhere to go
       the unjudging unforgiving sea if trees
       bare of leaf and memory
pig ignorant small survivals
difficult road making tasks
from frowsty theories and conceits

growing through a lack of answers
rubbled silo and milkweed
the mother moment seeps through boundaries
unmoored meaning exiled within a self
the oldest whom
the cold then the sleet of stars
dance in the bird dark thickets
hear the rutting badger cry
over the stubbled wake of sodden fields
laying the ash of grace
broken master of moonlight
fluxed into enduring void
where stars tell space-time how to bend
fallen apples tally fate
crows tell stars where to go
who allows who forbids
the individual refuses to hold together
eat bruised apples with your nose
swallow soaring birds with your eyes
unriddle the cinders of wings in your throat
the essential reality of lampposts
binds us to mortality
stray greasy cars in the rain
we who are now dying
in that far corner where our children age
a strange sleeping adam
who lay with himself
in a permanent dream of refuge denied
the sheer authority of seed
the thing known before it was known
black captivity between the ears
one ravenous one lenten eye
and the master of borrowed words

turns the apple-sucking snake round
with nightterms in the morning
       we are tired as the winds we wear
       footing the beacon of ash
across lowing fields
past empty webs in the barn door
rain starspilt impossibility
       life is too short for metaphysics
       wet crows scream from their universe
darkness is not evil
light is not good
they end only where they meet
       fringes of being are slipping out of words
       nostrils smoke in the rain
a crow calls
the universe laughs
an apple falls and the empire of our will trembles
       while evening lights come on
       the desperately wanted absolute haunts again
strewing the days with laughter
and what was broken and torn
come round in autumn twilight
       one is silent the other screams
       wild apples crows in the rain

Revisited January 22, 2014, for *Zen Encounters with Loneliness*
  T.K.

15

THE CANTICLE OF ECSTASY

Doing the world is doing what you are. Practice is realizing what you do, actualizing you, actualizing the world. It denies nothing. It is why I had to work through that clumsy poem, why it was necessary to stop being victimized by my addiction, by my choices. I am responsible for my life and that does not exclude anything. For me the image that has always expressed unhindered doing the world is the image of the wind.

When my children were small and I was home with them during the day, they often watched Sesame Street. One of the clips shown on the program from time to time was of a girl leaping down her stoop and dancing around in the wind to a song called "Windy Day." Whenever it came on the children would call out, "Pop! Pop! Come quick! Your Windy Day is on!" And I would come running from whatever I was doing to spend two or three minutes with them watching this girl toss her hair and twirl about in the wind.

My mother referred to "March manyweathers," and the phrase has always conjured up the wind in many forms, usually flashing clouds, hard ground, blue and grey whipping across the sky, laundry flapping, trees still bare but waking and speaking in the huge voice of the wind. The editor of my first book noted right away how often wind was a metaphor in my poems.

Is there anyone who has not thought that joy must be carefree, that it is freedom from the burdens of life, of self and others? It is not carefree. It is full of cares. It is everything. It is the windows of the heart thrown open willingly to the manyweathers of the world.

Red Tail

Where no reaching shade thorns the wind
nor coping rains charm from what fierce dreams
the sea-sounding sigh of dawn,
voice, in windy spaces,
the indecipherable clause of wings.

What is trust? Trust is not faith, though we often use it that way. People without any faith can trust enough to go to sleep at night. Lying in bed, thinly clothed, closing your eyes, letting go . . . in *this* world? What else if not trust? It takes other forms. In a talk once, the religious studies scholar Huston Smith made a distinction between what he called science and scientism. With the latter the deep need for light at the end of the tunnel allows good minds to want to trust vague answers to hopeful situations, making leaps of hope where there is none. Trust is fallible. There may be monsters under your metaphorical bed.

Most of us trust we are normal. What could normal possibly mean? Peace Pilgrim and monk Claude An Shin Thomas say, "Normal is the root of all war." How many wars have been fought to destroy those who are not normal by someone's arbitrary standards? Is such trust misplaced? Trust, commonly used, implies a value (we trust goodness, in God we trust), but it is actually an action. From a deepening meditative practice we learn to act appropriately and so we learn to trust appropriately. We learn to trust ourselves. Are we willing to let go to sleep tonight? Can we then let go to wake up?

When you look into a puddle—St. Nadie's mirror—the rippling world reflected back to you has no maps. How can you find the way if you trust enough to let go and enter the mirror of No One? It takes the patience of plants, the trust of trees awaiting the wind to blow seeds. It takes the happiness of others becoming your own as you stand, face upward with the trees. What do you see when you look away from St. Nadie's mirror? Are the old maps any good anymore?

I know I will die. So do you. Can you live with that knowledge? Do you have a choice? Is mortality a gift? A pointless question. Still, another day of life—what luck! The odds are against us. There is no moment in a town this size when someone is not dying, but the blue winds race by our upturned faces anyway. How do we reconcile this? How many deaths? No, how many breaths? How many children dancing in the wind? How many stertorously breathing old women with no one to moisten dry cracked lips? I know I will die. I know I live. I will breathe them all.

My dreams are only human dreams. They come from a boy in an old style woolen winter coat, a rusty plaid rough on his chin, in a broken cornfield under the wind. I knew it then but I had no words nor did I need any. When I needed them I began to forget ("down they forgot as up they grew") what I knew. But I did not really forget, for the winds have come round, have hollowed me out. Can you trust it? Can you taste it?

The three active virtues that are the source of joy resonate like bell sounds carried on the wind. I can no longer tell from which direction they emanate—for it is from every direction—with no exception *no blame*, always without hesitation *be kind*, and regardless of conditions *love everything* unconditionally. There is always a child running in the wind.

Part VI

THE THREE INFINITIES

16

INFINITE GRATITUDE TO THE PAST

What is the Zen life? When Huston Smith asked this question of a Rinzai Zen master in Japan, after a week-long arduous sesshin, anxious to discover why one would work so hard at practice, he was told: the Zen life is infinite gratitude for all that is past; infinite service toward all that is present; and infinite responsibility toward all that is in the future.

Letter to Hayden Carruth (that self-proclaimed unknown presence in the hills and creature of oblivion):

Dear Hayden,
As usual, it's early morning and everyone else is asleep. It seems a good time to hold certain kinds of conversation, the kind in which the past and other burdens of mortality come in between the lines. The cats are gathering around hoping I've cranked up the heat. This old house creaks in its sleep and the cold dark without presses in, deepening the silence of everything but my restless mind. I imagine you awake too in your even older house out in the boonies, though for you the sleepless hours have been long and I'm just an early riser. I sense you with coffee and cigarettes at your desk, avoiding your own reflection in the winter black window, the valley beyond invisible and infinite before dawn.

I've known you for close to twenty years. In that time we've each come through the worst: your suicide [attempt] and your daughter's death, my crushing addiction and illness. Though it hasn't been a close knowing, it's been friendly enough and has become warmer in some way in recent years. Perhaps the warmth comes from my approaching the age when you began to grouse about being old and your approaching the age when you really are old and have something to grouse about. But I think the real reason is we've come to recognize fellow exiles; a shared fondness for ruins—in ourselves, in others, in things and in places; and a common sense of the intractability of time and the seeming hopelessness of our equally intractable determination to transcend it. We each have tried, with mixed reviews, to make our own ways.

One of my most treasured possessions is a little grey book, *One Hundred Poems from the Chinese*, translated by Kenneth Rexroth. It was given to me when I turned twenty by the first girl I ever loved. Each year I go to it for solace, wisdom, a cleanliness of spirit—especially to the poems of Tu Fu. When you published *A Summer with Tu Fu* I felt suddenly privileged to be sitting in on an intimate chat between two old favorite uncles, who could look at me in a kindly way from time to time, wondering what stupid thing I would do next. You write:

> See how the heron folds her neck
> in flight. See how mysteriously she perches
> on the dead willow in her heraldic silence.
>
> After all perhaps we are the same. Who can
> the master be, who the apprentice? We embrace,
> two smiling old men standing on the end of a pier.

Life is not blind chance. We are at home in the universe.

Although we had met a few times before, our first real conversation, over dinner at your place, was about cows. No one believes me when I tell them it was one of the best discussions on poetry I've ever had. It had to do with hard work, attention to detail, the blessing of routine and its burden ("Cows don't take no vacations," as Jane's late dairy farming uncle used to say). It was about the nature of nature, not the pastoral romantic version of it, but nature in its unforgiving actuality about which we have to write clearly and truly. I have had to outgrow my own romance with the visionary. You have helped, a skeptical, even reluctant mystic, claiming disinterest in "that Asian bullshit," yet talking with affection to Tu Fu; an exile in his own country and a spiritual fugitive; homeless and in love with home; a man alone who cannot put people aside.

I once asked a friend, a soil conservationist who lives out in the Finger Lakes, what the name of the lake on which he lived meant. It has a lovely Iroquois name, Canandaigua, and I assumed it must embody a profound spiritual sensibility about the lake. It did but not in the way I expected. "It means," he said, "the place where we are." That is the clarity you have brought to your writing about the world around you. Not a bad model. So talking about cows was better than talking about iambs and was the beginning of what friendship we have.

I was moved by your story of how Mark Van Doren, in the time of your deepest poverty and exile, appeared in your farmhouse kitchen just to see you, just to tell you he admired your poems. That precious validation and big-heartedness must have come like breath to the drowning. Somehow it reminds me of a story about Pasternak. Late in his life, long after he had survived the deaths of such friends as Mandelstam at the hands of Stalin, many years into his own internal exile and enforced official neglect, he was giving a rare public reading. The auditorium was packed with thousands of people (unthinkable numbers in our culture; we do not censor artists, we ignore them, banish them with our silence to isolation, exile, and despair). At one point, in the middle of a poem he accidentally knocked his sheaf of papers to the floor. Interrupting himself, he stooped to retrieve his poems. A voice in the audience rose, taking up Pasternak's lines where he'd left off. Other voices joined the one. Soon the entire auditorium was resonating with the poem chanted back to the poet. Pasternak stood there, papers hanging from his hand at his side, tears rolling down his face. The community in which we may affirm one another's calling is small, perhaps, but you have taught me the value of nurturing it.

There is, too, the larger community of giving. Do you know Neruda's story of how, when he was a boy in Temuco, a rough town in the rainy, fertile south of Chile, he came across a hole in his back yard fence? And of how another, unseen boy pushed through the hole a small, much used stuffed toy lamb? And how Neruda pushed back, as a return gift, a much treasured resinous pine cone? He writes:

> People whom we love are a fire that feeds our lives. But to feel the affection that comes from those whom we do not know . . . that is something still greater and more beautiful because it widens out the boundaries of our being and unites us with all living beings.

You have a tough way of reminding people of this. I recall once at a dinner someone made a comment about the Ward brothers. It wasn't meant to be condescending, observing the sadness of their poverty and their not knowing how to get out of it. One of the brothers had died and another was accused of murdering him. The entire village and farming community came out in their defense, feeling that not only did they not understand what was being done to them but that they were people incapable of killing. You jumped on the speaker, making clear that "the boys," as they were known, lived perfectly happy in a style common a century ago and that they didn't need our judgment or values to get on with their lives. By their own standards, they managed to live well enough to keep the farm working and to get by, more than can be said for many family farms trying to meet other standards closer to our own levels of hygiene and materialism. Your comment was also a kind of giving, a returning of the dignity of being without judgment or conditions.

Unlike you, I am not a compulsive worker, though when friends hear about how I spend my time they would disagree, what with teaching, collection development, and committee work at the university library; the chaplaincy, pastoral care, and counseling work; contributions to the Zen Center; volunteer work with the Inter-religious Council's Native American Task Force; not to mention my family's needs and my own for writing and painting. Maybe I am too Irish, but I always felt the Protestant work ethic, that work itself was somehow morally good, a wrong-headed pain in the ass.

However, much like you, I have also felt the need to accomplish what was necessary—job, duties, commitments to family—before I took the privileged time away to write. Yeats wrote somewhere that one had to choose between the work (the art) or the life. I have spent my life defying that, trying to make the work of art and the work of life both true without excluding one or the other. I don't know if you feel the price you paid to accomplish this too was worth it, but I would pay the price of exhaustion, illness, and addiction over and over if I could have my beautiful, sane, happy children, the sustaining love of my wife, and one poem that opened the heart of another being.

You have written on art and reality:

> Nothing in an interposed medium can be the thing itself. Our lives in art, whether we make it or respond to it, are centered precisely on dumb futility, the way of being is centered on nothingness. We who make art must know this and must inform those who are the responders. We must do it repeatedly. Otherwise art is all sham and mendacity, and neither truth nor beauty can come from it.

You have said that you and the three generations of modernists were too successful, that there is nothing new that can be done in poetry now—that this always happens at the end of an era. But don't you see, we are now at a place where there are no names, no maps, no descriptions. Our duty is now to express what is unheard of.

You wrote in "The Sleeping Beauty":

Third is the poem, who must make
Presence from words, vision from seeing,
This no one that uniquely in sorrow rejoices
And can have no pronoun.

I wrote in "Black Honey":

How do I know you are speaking to me
when there are no words, no signs,
just the ordinary magic of two people
for whom silence is both grief and joy?
When you say, "Listen! The wind!"
You are already wind in the trees.
If there is an alternative,
I don't know what it is.

Suddenly I shiver in the cold of the house. I put down my pen and smell my hands before my face. It is my own smell, something I have carried with me more than fifty years. Can I then speak only for myself? What a pitiful thought. You are the first person to have said, so far as I know, "At a tender age I was taught to fear myself and the least promotion of myself." I can't tell you what a relief that shock of recognition was for me, for I too had it reinforced again and again. My response and struggle out of it have been different from yours, but no less difficult. I still relapse into that withering self-consciousness from time to time, but it is part of the reason I fought to keep art and life together. Tu Fu wrote, "The moonlight / means nothing to the soldiers / camped on the western deserts." The moonlight cannot intrinsically "mean" to anyone. Meaning is the nostalgic fiction we make of reality. Neither you nor I "mean," nor does what we do. Nothing led inexorably to us and we do not lead inexorably to anything. What a relief! At last there is no one there to fear nor to be fearful.

I think we have tried to write toward a kind of wellness, trying against all odds to maintain the velocity of our passion for living despite all the outside forces working on it, as you have described it. Wellness. Being whole. Being wholly empty of the divided, divisive self, being, as you say, "a duck blown out to sea and still squawking."

It's still dark, though I have to start moving to get breakfast ready for everyone. We have our different lives, memories and losses. Two yellow lamps in windows on the dark. The cold goes on forever and is deeper than light or warmth. But we sit here in the silence, unshaven, stiff. What light there is shines into the past; past us, past the yellow dust of kings and courtesans and bone strewn battlefields of Tu Fu's vanished empire, past the ages of beast and ice, past the past. Without all of it we could not be here to grouse, to laugh, to love. We are not worthy in ourselves, but in that to which we give rise. I, for one, am grateful, old man, for your poems and for your life which have both opened my heart more than once. No blame, be kind, love everything.

Fondly,
terry

Infinite Gratitude to the Past

The ravaged road goes on and on
in both directions.
Who can I ask to buy the bones?

Snow settles on hemlock and yew.
This is enough
to the end of my days
without end amen.

17

INFINITE SERVICE TO THE PRESENT

I know nothing
I cannot speak
But these are my tears
Upon your cheek
—Jim Bogan

When I used to wake with night sweats my mind would spin in endless loops of anxiety, going over little irresolvable problems like a miser counting pennies, unable to stop, to sleep. Even when I told myself there was truly nothing to worry about and believed it, still, the wild worries persisted. The ghosts of these attacks haunted me for years.

Sometimes it's okay. Sometimes it's not one desperate act after another. Sometimes we hear the music that is always there. As the old Irish homily goes: "The most beautiful music is the music of what happens." It is not necessary to run to a remote, quiet place to hear it. It is here already, always. The essence of eternity is how we experience the present. The witnesses are here in ourselves. The fullness of our inheritance denies nothing.

Our home is on the east side of the city at the bottom of a hill. It was once part of the nearby suburb, but was incorporated a few decades ago. In our downstairs bathroom, which was papered by a former owner with newspapers from the year the house was built in the late twenties, there is a real estate ad for: "Bradford Hills, where City meets Country." It is still true, though there is a steady flow of traffic nearby that would have been unimaginable in 1928. We have a large wood lot behind us and have seen deer, pheasant, and even a wild turkey. Once raccoons nested in our chimney for a couple of seasons. Rabbit, skunk, muskrat, groundhog (wonderful names!) and the usual array of squirrels (including many black ones) and birds are all commonplace visitors. Our understanding is not needed. To be aware is a simple kind of prayer. These beings help our awareness in a city by plying their lives around us in spite of us.

Most days, when my wife and I come home from work, we fall into a routine as I get supper ready and the cats fed. Every once in a while something happens, like those moments at a party when everyone stops talking at once. Suddenly there is an audible silence in both of us. It is, perhaps, a grey winter evening. Snow has fallen much of the day so that the familiar world is momentarily masked. Our senses are curiously alight and, in tune with one another's, become aware not of the sameness of things caused by the covering of snow but by the spectacular particularity, the suchness of each thing.

The sun drops below the cloud cover, flashes gold and rose on the snow. The slanting light fills the room. The neighbor's roof and the tops of the trees in the back suddenly glow with new fire so each old shingle, each sleeping frozen twig is expressed completely. We simply stand together, arms around each other's waist. The easiness is right there, no effort at all. When we are truly human the ethical life, the religious life, and the ordinary life are the same in this simple, easy way. When we ask, only silence prevails. There is no response, for in this complete moment we are our own answer: we dwell in empty freedom nevertheless.

But lest we get smug—and speaking of the house next door—who can say the stars have not left their regular course unnoticed? This winter that house went up on the tax auction block for the third time. Twice the owner had found a way to keep his home. This time he lost it. And if it hadn't been this time, there would have been another, for he is hopelessly in debt and has never been able to cope with even the basic fiscal responsibilities of home ownership. I doubt he ever knew how—or even what they were.

The house is the same 1920s vintage as ours, well-made, good materials. There is a beautiful, craggy sugar maple in the front lawn that is one of the glories of the neighborhood, especially in October. The house looks like no one has lived in it for ten years. Indeed, while we've been out working in our gardens, people have stopped and asked if anyone lives there, could it possibly be for sale? Plantings are wildly overgrown. Foxgrape has destroyed the hedge by the main road. The lawn more often looks like a fallow field than a lawn. An elderly neighbor (who signs her acerbic admonitions to various neighbors about trash and other protocols "the Neighborhood," and so we all refer to her as the Neighborhood, as in "The Neighborhood says . . .") has had a busy time calling the police frequently each summer to complain about our neighbor's unkempt yard. The owner of the messy property will then go out and cut it in a huff, only to leave it another six weeks.

When we moved here, he was living with his mother and grandmother, the latter of whom owned the house and kept it in fair repair. She died a couple of years later, but his mother kept the place up, if a little less fastidiously. It seems she and her son were herbalists and had any number of curious plants growing among the evergreens. Not everything was a weed. He gave us occasional lectures on how much he disliked cutting or killing plants. But then his mother died.

The DA showed up to investigate, which caused a lot of neck-craning up the street, but everything turned out okay, if sad and lonely for the son, their two dogs and several cats, all of whom (including the son) remained almost entirely house-bound. Year by year things went downhill. The detached garage filled, literally filled, with empty beer bottles. Until the winter he lost the place. He grew up there. Now he is "temporarily" living at the Y. There is a pattern of learned helplessness here brought on by a collusion of economic, political, and social forces and by avoidance. He avoided what he needed to know and do; we and the entire community avoided his plight. Where will he go? Whom do we serve? We are not faceless. We wear our face and it is his face. It is confused by the absence of a model for ordinary life, the deepest confusion of our times. It is a face mortal and frail.

Service. Kindness. Duty. One Sunday, a while back, we were having an all-day sitting at the Zen Center. The normal Sunday sitting, which runs from nine to twelve, had been canceled and only those participating in the all-day sitting were expected to be there. In general, the atmosphere was more intense than that of a regular Sunday, a bit closer to sesshin. A few people ignored or didn't notice the cancellation sign on the door and came to sit anyway, as though it were a regular Sunday. When they realized that things were on a different schedule, or as they were spoken to by one of the *jisharyō* (the two *jisha*, or individuals responsible for caring for the sitters with motherly kindness), they either stayed on and participated fully or left quietly during the next walking meditation. There was one exception.

He would have been late regardless of what sort of sitting we were having. About twenty minutes into a period of zazen there was a noise on the stairs. The latecomer arrived without ceremony, with his sneakers still on (he also seemingly ignored the "please remove shoes" sign) and several noisy plastic shopping bags, holding water bottles and other paraphernalia. To those sitting he seemed unaware of the silence in the room, he proceeded to set up camp on one of the cushions in a back row, rattling bags, kicking off shoes. I, somewhat irritated, tried to help him and hauled away the shoes and some of the gear to an unobtrusive spot. When the period ended I drew him aside and explained the situation, about how we do things and that this was a special day, and so on. He gathered his things and left. What I did not know was that he was dying of cancer, that he came for succor and support, that he had a serious cold and needed all that gear to cope.

He said nothing and no one asked. Assumptions were made on both sides, but where was the extended hand of motherly kindness? Where were the ears that hear the cries of the world?

I may not have known and acted as I was expected and trained to act, without anger, but something was missed. It is a subtle matter, as our teacher would say. If we do not know and cannot know another's suffering, how can we be open to it? Openness is called emptiness, not fixating or holding on to anything, not even the *shoulds* of propriety. Pity and sympathy are not compassion but forms of desire—desire to help. There is an important tradition of urgency in Rinzai Zen practice (if not now, when?!), but not to the exclusion of compassion, giving, and witnessing without exclusion. Albert Schweitzer tells us, "The great enemy of morality has always been indifference." To remain good means to remain awake. He also says, "Existence depends more on reverence for life than the Law or the Prophets. Reverence for life comprises the whole ethic of love in its deepest and highest sense. It is the source of constant renewal for the individual and for mankind." Practice forever and let go of the teaching. Death has no more answers than life.

Compassion is the great intimacy—intimacy with the present. In addressing the Seventh Grave Precept (Realize self and other as one, do not elevate self and blame others) in *The Heart of Being,* Daido Loori Roshi puts it like this:

> When you realize in your life that cause and effect are one, you realize that what you do and what happens to you are the same thing. To see this clearly is to realize that each of us is responsible not only for ourselves and our lives but also for the whole phenomenal universe. Whatever happens to this great earth, this universe and its inhabitants, happens to each one of us. It is the same karma. When you realize that, there is no way to avoid taking responsibility for your life. There is no way to blame.

The experience of intimacy is most immediate, most *present*, in the relationship with one's teacher. Often we want our teachers to earn their sanctity in *our* currency. Is there a safe place in which we can be intimate without risk? Or do we put this risk as a burden on our teacher by demanding they affirm us in some way—in our way. *Dokusan* (formal private interview with one's teacher) can be more intimate than any place imaginable in any relationship. It is also the least risk-free place imaginable, if one is risking one's ego. It is an intimacy not unlike that of lovers, though without the sex, which is why students are vulnerable and teachers can get into trouble. My relationship with my teacher has not always been smooth.

There have been wounds, though I have never really questioned that it was a true relationship. Nor, I think, has she questioned it. We have both worked at it to make it work. It got pretty shaky, for example, during the Zen Center's transition from a small group of like-minded friends with a spiritual director to a solid functioning nonprofit organization, a church, so to speak, with an abbot. When we had to create a working budget and a policy to manage it, there were conflicts over authority and how to express the needs for change. But we resolved them. What ragged ego I have left (plenty, alas) has taken a real beating in dokusan, as it should. Some of my biggest problems have come in koan study. Not so much in the koans themselves, though they are quite demanding enough, but with the method or process of teaching and studying them. It has sometimes seemed to me, in my impulsive American way, that the method can be too formulaic, that the formal need to express a "correct" presentation of understanding can override the real one as experienced by the student. Can the Dharma ever be other than the Dharma? For a while they became meaningless games.

But I am slow to learn. Questioning the process is part of the process of learning to trust my own experience in its own truth—to "follow the light and take care of my own truth" (Barry Lopez, *Arctic Dreams*). To doubt is to be whole. To face your own face is to doubt everything blameworthy and affirming outside of yourself.

Trusting the truth of your doubt turns you back to participation in the process, inside it instead of merely observing it. One's teacher is a mirror for you to see yourself, with you always, in the wounded place and in the whole. There can be no blame; there, kindness takes infinite and unexpected forms; there, love is the responsibility and service and witness to all.

INFINITE SERVICE TO THE PRESENT

Nothing remote
about this house in the city in the snow,
but we dwell in empty freedom nevertheless.
Snow fills the drive and walk.
Subtle endless tones of grey all day.
At dusk the sun dips
below the western cloud cover
and last lights linger
on roof ridges and trees in the east.
Silence so sweet
even the hungry ghosts listen.

Every evening birds come to roost
on the house next door.
The beautiful old maple out front
is enough to sadden you to death.
No one has been seen at a window
in a long time.
The boy is now a confused man
left unprepared for the world,
its dues, burdens, and dust.
All lost in a tax auction
after three generations.
Where will he go?

No one asks her who she is
or how she got here
and she has forgotten herself.
My need is so great, she says,
I don't care what your problems are.
She is dying from death,
turning into haze and mist,
and the pain, well,
it burns up everything
even ash.
You don't know, she says,
who you are
or where you're going,
help me.

Sometimes a whisper, sometimes a roar,
without deficiency or condition—
why are you angry
when I cannot tell you its source?
Because I am dull and tongue-tied
does not mean
the light shines less brightly.
Are there exceptions?
These games are meaningless
and the need to show you
the source of my being
fades like winter stars at dawn.
You are with me always
in what is now
the wounded place and the whole,
our breath visible in the cold air.

18

INFINITE RESPONSIBILITY TO THE FUTURE

For Father's Day, my son gave me a mix CD that he had burned himself. We've been doing this with tapes for years. On the CD was a song by Ani DiFranco, one of his favorite singer/songwriters, called "I'm not angry anymore." It is heartbreaking for me to listen to it. It is his way of saying he has finally come to some sort of peace with my being an alcoholic. What was bitter is over ("now I know what all the fighting was for"). What is heartbreaking is the knowledge of the years of hurt I've brought him and that I can't take any of it back, that he was angry for so long—so angry for so long that he had to find a way to tell me he wasn't like that anymore.

He was the one who took my relapses and slips in the early years the hardest. When my wife backed off, he became my policeman and conscience, especially since I timed my slips for when his mother was out of town. A big job for a (then) little kid. This change toward forgiveness comes at an apt moment. He has been home from college where he got his first taste of being his own man. At home he is still our child, albeit a grown one. He has found the role frustrating. As parents everywhere must, I am letting him go now into his own life. As parents everywhere do, I do so with difficulty, but also with the knowledge that he is an independent and forgiving human being and that we have come of age as men together.

When we are responsible for someone or something, it is with our imperfections that we live that responsibility. He carries my imperfect lessons of an imperfect life down the street, into the snow, out of my time and place and meaning. Meaning is the memory, the words describing the life we experienced together. It is the *practice* of life, his own life, that is the direct experience of reality I hope he takes along the road I cannot go down. As he goes, I wonder what his children seven generations hence will be like? His life makes me ask why and how I swerved from my own life, from my responsibilities to him, which are at the core of life itself. Moonsnares, foxwords, the self-deceptive fictions we carry through time, become so familiar we wish we could attribute to them the happiness and joy and living they deny us. And yet they come from and are part of who we are.

Words from Tu Fu come back to haunt me:

> All creatures pursue happiness.
> Why have I let an official
> Career swerve me from my goal?

And:

> The mountain pears are tiny but ripe.
> A Tartar flute plays by the city gate.
> A single wild goose climbs into the void.

What does "infinite responsibility" mean? Iris Murdoch says, "We would like to know what, as moral agents, we have got to do because of logic; what we have got to do because of human nature; and what we can choose to do." Taking responsibility empowers us to accept we cannot know everything. History has meaning only in the mutable present. The responsibility to the future must show our profound embeddedness in the web of life. That very realization of embeddedness can relieve us of our arrogance and loneliness. I am not worthy in myself, but in that to which I have given rise—this single wild goose climbing into the void.

Infinite Responsibility to the Future

What possible meaning
could birds have
flocked to an old chimney
in late afternoon
as my son takes the car
down the street and into the snow?
Without this moment
nothing else will happen.
Beloved moonsnares and foxwords
everything is incomprehensible
now and then.

PART VII

BLUE HEAPED UPON BLUE

19

WHAT WE CAN'T TALK ABOUT

Overwhelming evening clouds
gathering in one great mass.
Endlessly arising distant mountains,
blue heaped upon blue.
—FROM *Setcho's Verse*, CASE 20, HEKIGANROKU
(EIDO SHIMANO ROSHI'S TRANSLATION)

Only lies wear a tongue smooth. I take a walk on a cold evening, wondering how to step back from my own mind. The crunch of snow under my boots creates a rhythm and a background noise so that I am alone with my thoughts, undistracted. The only mind I can know firsthand is my own. I infer others exist because there is no reason not to and experience makes sense of it. I have no direct access to other minds and can manage only through language and image to connect at all. The privacy of the mind, a curse and a blessing. Matter and mind are nothing ultimate, but merely ordering concepts. Buddhism does not talk about the differences between mind and matter. And so it goes, round and round, as I go round and round the block in the cold starry dark, my smooth-tongued consciousness, my wanting grace to arrive, like Aesop's grasshopper, like Joyce's Gracehoper, singing my own song and hoping my proclivity for mistakes does not mark me forever.

Many people curse the Meiji government of nineteenth-century Japan for allowing monks (but not nuns?) to marry, breaking, thereby, some of the power and influence of the great monasteries in politics. As monks focused on local temples and family affairs they were less involved with monastic futures. Frankly, I'm glad it happened or I could not be in the position I am in. There are those outside of Japan who say *real* monks practice celibacy and there are those inside of Japan who say *real* monks must spend a specific length of time in a monastery. What interests me more than whether monks are real is whether monks, however we define them, practice *real* life and live a responsible, loving life in a family. It is complicated for most Buddhist clergy in our culture because, except for the Pure Land sect, there is no substantial infrastructure to support the livelihood of the clergy.

In other words, I cannot earn a living as a monk or a priest. I must do something else to contribute to the household, like hold a full-time paying job and still do "clergy stuff," as one friend put it: lead services and sittings, do pastoral care in hospitals, help perform funeral services, give counseling and talks and so on, and be on interfaith councils and committees—or be the token non-Judeo-Christian representative on any number of panels or gatherings. If I am also to do well in my day job, it makes for a busy and complicated life. I may once have been motivated by "The Fool on the Hill," but life has shown me to be a fool of another sort—a very busy one. When we, as a family, discussed what we thought were the implications of my ordination, none of us realized how much it would involve for each of us. I became absorbed before I knew what was happening or what it might be doing to the family fabric. Sometimes as a family we have to pause, call a H.A.L.T. (Hungry, Angry, Lonely, Tired) meeting, and get back on track. It just takes one of us for the whole family system to be askew. But we are getting better at seeing the signs, braver at saying, "Hey, we need to talk."

In Ray Carver's faithful and bitter book of stories, *What We Talk About When We Talk About Love*, one of the more obvious things the reader discovers is that we don't, we can't, talk about love and we will talk about just about anything else. In our family we have had to learn to talk about love. It is like talking about joy. The loss, the need, the longing, the betrayal, the obsession, and so on, sure. Every country and western station in the land plays songs about such things all day long, and libraries are full of fiction and poetry attesting to the same. But what about four people sitting around a table who love one another very much? Perhaps it is less what we cannot say than what cannot be said at all. Sometimes it is just how we are with one another. Even that, by itself, is not simple. The family dynamic is made up of complex layers, for how we experience and express our love, each for another, is different from one to the other. In our family several extra layers of complexity were added with how my addiction affected the dynamic, how each member responded not only to me but to one another in that context. No wonder Carver wrote that we can't find what we need to say.

When I vow to give my life to the sangha, it is not an abstract statement, an offering to some idealized collective. It begins here at home, and only from here can I open my heart to the larger community. It begins with trust. Unconditional trust has always been an important piece for us. I betrayed that trust to the family and to each individual. As a group and as individuals they all responded to the betrayal differently. It may not have been willful on my part. I didn't choose to be an alcoholic, but obviously there were behaviors in which I engaged that served my addiction first before they served my family or my vocations.

The one place I could always turn to express my love for them was in my poetry. I couldn't lie there. This did not serve my addiction so much as it did my ego vision. Until close to the end when I could hardly string a coherent sentence together, poetry was my last resort for honesty. My grandfather always held that real art could never be dishonest. I still think that's true. Not everyone in the family felt that way. Borges says of Shakespeare that he was someone who adopted "the habit of feigning that he was somebody, so that his nobody-ness might not be discovered." I was feigning I was no one in order to hide that I thought I was someone.

I was often deeply hurt when my wife would dismiss or ignore poems I would give her. Later I learned she thought they were manipulative, that after some incident caused by my drinking, my giving her a poem was an attempt to coerce her into not taking the incident too seriously. In counseling I explained the need to tell her the truth that I couldn't normally, that poetry was my only means around my self-justifying behavior, and that by rejecting it I was losing the last hope and vestige of clarity I had available to me. I think we were both surprised by what the other had thought, so far apart had we become. And so far from reality had *I* become. I had held on too long to my grandfather's vision. Even writing about it now I over use "I" and recognize the old fear of loneliness when I don't.

Of course, it is easy, as I've noted, to write about the difficulties of love. It has not all been horrible, by any means, or my wife and I could not have managed thirty-one years together.[4] One area of our lives that is different and that is perhaps most central to my role as a monk is our shared practice. I am not her teacher (or anyone else's, for that matter), nor is she mine. It would be unfair to our long intimacy as lovers to burden it with the equally deep but distinct intimacy of teacher and student. Even my own teacher's husband practices in the Tibetan tradition and has his own teacher. It *has* been a test of our personal relationship, at times, when we move through and express our practice in different ways. Sometimes my wife and I feel one should be like the other, that we should keep a tally to make sure we're keeping up with one another, able to "arrive" together. Some of that comes from our courting days.

I recall vividly the day we crossed the frontier from boyfriend/girlfriend to lovers for life. We were sitting on a log over a nameless stream one spring day, swinging our legs, laughing in each other's company. We looked up at one point and just knew something had happened.

4. As of this edition our forty-fifth anniversary is fast approaching.

Like the student who admits he knows nothing suddenly opens the doors to all things, we let go our striving to be something to or for the other. We just let go and opened our hearts. It is a heart-to-heart transmission for which there are no real words. Anyone who has fallen in love knows this. It cannot be proven empirically, but we know it is so.

Mind-to-mind transmission is a similar experience. When I am asked how I could possibly believe in this mind-to-mind hocus-pocus, I respond by asking if the questioner was ever in love. Did you ever feel the person in the room before you actually saw them there? Ever know what they were thinking without being told, even when not in the same room? Ever find all the poems and songs inadequate to the experience of open trust of this heart-to-heart transmission? Ever just know you're both in love without words, gestures, explanations? Usually they can, if they have been in love, answer yes to at least some of these questions, especially the last. Even if they have not been in love, they will acknowledge that it is a true human experience others have had.

Pema Chödrön writes of the teacher-student relationship like this:

> You're encouraged to have passionate involvement with life—with love, illness, death, disappointment. There is no emotion or activity that is off limits as a source of wisdom.

Or of love, one might add. This is not to make of these relationships, either that of lovers or that of teachers and students, something mystical or otherworldly. They are palpable, real. Whatever biological need or evolutionary process from which they may have emerged, they are true human experiences, perhaps the most intense and important of the many human experiences for which we have no words to affirm. When my wife and I were courting, I expressed it that there could be no other love, that we looked through the same eyes toward the light. I used to think we both felt that way.

I kept an iron grip on that romantic dream of shared vision. It made things messy and complicated later on. It prevented me from allowing my wife her own growth and discovery on her own terms. It had to be on these shared terms, through the same eyes, which of course became over time *my* eyes. It was some time into my recovery, after we had renewed our lives together, that I began to revel in her practice, take joy in her experiencing her practice, and so her life, on her terms. I had been too thick before to see how that could enrich our lives now. I had to drop something to be able to enter her life, but I refused to see what.

There is a bitter aftertaste when one swallows the truth, sometimes. It may be years before it becomes apparent, so long as you've forgotten that first taste, but it does come. It comes when, having thought you swallowed truth whole, what you got was only a morsel. Further, the spreading bitterness derives from understanding that what you thought was true was, actually, true, but not in the way you thought or wanted it to be. So it was with my poetry. I believed and still believe completely that real art cannot lie. What I am only beginning to understand is that I impose my own conditional smooth-tongued truths upon it, thinking them to come from the art, and finding the poems and me empty when I realize they do not. Was it still a gift to others when I took myself out of the poems?

My wife once told me of an afternoon idyll while we were canoeing. She had paddled and floated around a duck marsh for hours, letting the water take her, no plans, no real thoughts even, just floating, trailing her hand in the water. Suddenly she apprehended the answer to Bassui's ancient question, "Who is it who hears?" She has carried the experience into other moments and it has become part of her strength. Seeing her unfold in her own life is the sweetness of loving without condition.

She Tells Him How Now She Is Rearranged

This sadness, tears, this vulnerability
       are shock waves of the hurt.
What was my hurt?

I still look around me
       in every direction.
What is my fear?

I dream that everywhere I go
       there is no one to support me.
What is my need?

Who am I when November winds
       spread over the grey hills
sing in my nest of bones?

Who is it trails my hand
       from the drifting canoe
in north lake waters?

I am the answer and the water
       and the wind.

20

TRYING TO BE LOVE

Mostly I was a happy drunk. My children used to call it my "fly away mood" before the days when they had any idea what was going on. I drank for a feeling of openness and ease, something I did not often experience normally, though I've always been fond of the goofy and offbeat. Sometimes I felt life was taking away opportunities to be lighthearted. Who hasn't felt that weight at one time or another? I did not want to drown my sorrows, but to draw back out to the light a happier, brighter me. The fact that my family stopped trusting that part of me as having anything to do with reality was a very long time in coming to me.

Of course, I was not always drinking, nor, when I drank, was I always drunk. Though, in the odd twists of addiction, I began to distrust the happy times when I *wasn't* drinking as somehow unreal. Nevertheless, save for the last year or so of my drinking I was usually not stoned or drinking, but just more or less normal me, whatever that was. The crippling, personality-changing behaviors of the addiction were many years in developing (though I never saw my increased tolerance as a symptom of the growing problem) and only became completely debilitating in the last two. I was once capable of laughing at myself and my circumstances, and of delighting in the wonder my children brought to the world. I was blessed with the opportunity to be with them during their very early years and so have a connection fathers don't always have.

My daughter was born in the dark end of November, just after Thanksgiving. There was snow in the air. Throughout the long hours of my wife's labor at home and in the hospital I held on to the demeanor of the helpful clinician and mate, efficient, ready, loving. There was some concern we did not voice because the labor was a month early. I did not want to add to my wife's effort and discomfort by getting frantic myself with anxiety over a premature birth. Perhaps, too, I was so stunned by the reality of the forthcoming birth that the only way I could cope myself was to take on completely the masking role of the good nurse-mate. Both of us had been good students in the Lamaze natural childbirth classes. We had to use everything we were taught and my wife had to draw on reserves of strength and tolerance for pain neither of us knew she had.

In the delivery room I sat at her head holding her hands, offering encouraging words, breathing with her in the rhythmical way we'd been taught. I did as I was told by the kindly but efficient Dr. Schorr and the nurses. When the tiny, wrinkled little creature emerged, accompanied by huge shouts of pain and effort, she was hardly bigger than my hand. But she was all there. The doctor placed her on my wife's chest and had me guide her hand to cut the umbilical cord. The doctor then said, "She is now an independent human being."

I began to tremble all over and burst into tears. The momentousness of this most normal human and animal experience flooded through me, through us both, all the clinical facade washing away in amazement at the life before us. Despite her exhaustion, my wife sensed it all more deeply than I ever could, flesh of her flesh. The nurse took baby-girl Keenan away for a moment to weigh her and clean her up. She was just a couple of ounces above the incubator stage. When they brought her back, all wrapped up, I gazed into her wide-open, bottomless eyes and wondered from where she had come into our lives? What did she already know that I would never know?

After two months maternity leave, my wife returned to work. I took over the feeding and changing responsibilities. There is a photo of me in my bookstore taken by a student at the college, a Diane Arbus wannabe. I'm looking drawn and tired, hair like an ill-fitting periwig, holding this tiny creature in the crook of my arm. There is an air of pain and desperation in the image, created by the badgering questions of the photographer, which had nothing to do with the reality of holding my child. This is not to say I did not curse the hours of walking around the shop and apartment (next to the shop) at night during her colicky third month, trying to get her to sleep, or that everything was always wonderful on the surface—though, amazingly, it was mostly so. We developed over the years, my daughter and I, an intuitive bond, the sort in which verbal communication is nearly superfluous. All through her childhood and adolescence that bond was part of who and what we were.

I betrayed that bond. Not deliberately, not even consciously, in that I could not imagine, because I could not see it happening, how my changing behavior affected her. When I came to a place in my healing and recovery where I could accept that I could not undo what had been done, I returned to an old poem I had written for her as a toddler. It went through many revisions as I tried to understand what had been lost and what we had left. Central to the poem was the sweet song of the wood thrush on summer evenings, an invisible deep beauty, rare, brief, emerging from our beloved woods. To me it recalls, each time I hear it, the mystery of her eyes at birth, the persistent yet hidden fragility of life and love. I imagined myself in a meadow on the hills above our village and somehow reaching to her in her young sleep in that intuitive way we reached one another, both of us somehow hearing the haunting fluting of the thrush. When I rewrote the poem, she was already a young woman. All I can tell her is that we are mortal and that I have struggled with mortality. It is where we both begin and it is the place where I can give only what I have, my flawed but earnestly lived life. Perhaps in the woods we each love so deeply she will discover for herself what I have been unable to find. It is my song of regret and of love.

WOODTHRUSH
—*for Bryna*

Each place is the end of the world.
This is the sound of what remains
out across long dusk,
your small fist of sleep in my hand
where a plain brown bird sounds
from the deepwood.

The tiny irreparable damage of living
is what I have given you.
By this sound be initiated
and see deeply.

Do not forget the myth of your body
for I once forgot mine
and the monk without faith
slept better than I.

Perhaps you will find what ruled me
after I am dead, for its fires
are still dark to me.

It is not skill, knowledge, intellect,
good luck or bad, but choosing
to feel the strange notes of our wildness,

for there is not nothingness
despite the easy magic of despair.

Read these woodsigns
hidden beyond the first steps
and regain our love in this sound.
Roads will never be closed to you.

We stand in a meadow of fireflies and timothy.
The sky lies pale with some stars.

The first thing my son did in the early seconds of life, while resting on his exhausted mother's abdomen, was to pee in the nurse's face. All his life he has managed to pull off a vigorous unexpected turn to things. As is often the way in the world, the deep intuitive bond he made was with his mother. As his mother's response to the world is always a source of surprise and wonder to me, so is his. It is different from his mother's but somehow connected; they accept their indigenous unpredictability in a way those outside the energy connecting them can only puzzle over and think amazing.

By the time his mother's maternity leave was up, I had sold my bookshop and was teaching adults at night in the local community college. This allowed me to be home all day with the children. But my son had his sister to keep him company much of the time, so our own intimate time was of a different order from what I experienced with his sister as a first-time parent. Yet, while he was in a sense more creatively independent of me than his sister, he felt the betrayal my drinking brought to our basic trust more bitterly than his sister did.

In the years I was trying to make amends I had to find a different way back to him. My daughter did not seem to question her intrinsic value the way he did. His perfect pitch that allowed him to memorize his Suzuki piano lessons on one hearing, or his skill even as a child in solving complex design problems that had important designers expressing admiration, he dismissed as inconsequential. He saw himself as something else and fought to have me see it too.

This was born out by an experience he related from an arduous canoe trip he had taken. It had been a tough day of long portages and inadequate maps, forcing the small group to bushwhack through raw wilderness for hours on end, loaded with canoes and gear. Finally in camp, after a lakeside meal, he was standing, listening, too tired to think. The small waves of the lake lapped the rocks. He sensed that these waves would be lapping the shore whether he was there or not. The door in his heart opened a crack. Suddenly, in letting himself go in this simple, unconscious way, he was flooded with an overwhelming sense of wholeness, realizing he *was* the waves, he *was* the lake, the wilderness, the universe.

He knew the story of my wanting to talk to God all day. He knew that is why I wrote poems and went to the monastery. When he told me this story he did not know something in me broke, and a crack opened in me also. His presence was not the grace of my former failures. I realized with shame that by now the god I wanted to talk to all day was me.

One winter at Rohatsu sesshin I stood in the gloaming snowy woods of Dai Bosatsu mountain. The scouring power of fourteen hours a day of meditation and discipline were having their effect. I was thinking of my son so intently it was as though he stood beside me in the snow. How could I show him my unjudging love, that I understood. This poem came:

Becoming the Mountain
—for Conor

They stood on a road in December.
Wind made snow ghosts among the trees.
The child asked, "Where does the wind come from?"

It comes from the mouth of nowhere,
between day and dark
so the trees can talk together.

"But it's winter now
and the trees are sleeping."

Yes, so listen carefully
to their dreams.

"And suppose I am the wind?"

Then you are also the dreams.

We change. This is a truism so blatant we could laugh at it, if we really believed it. We know *things* change, both things as circumstances and things as objects. The meadow across from the house where I grew up, which seemed like it had been there forever, has been filled with houses for forty years. To the people living in those homes the meadow, the games, and egg hunts were never there. Only their own memories are there. In our heart of hearts, however, most of us harbor a deep belief, so deep we accept it without thinking, that some part of us, an essential us, remains the same, regardless of events or even memories. It's an illusory belief. Is there nothing that holds? No. Nothing. No one. Nada. Nadie. Even if we hold what seem to be the same feelings and thoughts years later? Isn't there something essential in them that holds? No.

I discovered this the hard way. Perhaps it is the only way. We each have, I suppose, our own hard ways. During the time, as our twenty-fourth wedding anniversary approached, when our marriage was unraveling quickly, a time about which I have already written, I knew I still loved my wife. I felt certain there was some timeless element in this continued loving, perhaps just the loving itself, that I needed to understand to see where we'd gone wrong.

In the first couple of years of our marriage I wrote and revised often a poem, still in my Dylan Thomas phase, that I then thought captured the blazing divine light of our love for one another. I thought its exquisite sweetness was captured in the sweetness of wild timothy grass, which we both loved so much we named one of our first cars Timothy. Looking back on the poem a quarter century later, rather dazed and wounded from the crisis we had just survived, I realized I had wanted to *make* our love for one another somehow eternal, to fix it in some way in a timeless firmament so its power and purpose would carry us through all travail, and the world could stand in awe of its rightness. This is not to dismiss those young passions. When you are twenty-one and feel immortal, it's okay to love like an immortal. It remains however, a manipulation.

If I still loved her, even though the loving was troubled, twenty-five years later, was it the same love? No. I was not the same, nor was she. What I had come to know was that love was not a *thing* to have, to give, to receive. Love is an action, a way of being in the world and the moment. Only you can act for you; no one else will take that first loving step for you. The second part of the poem shows perhaps the first halting steps of an unmade man trying to *be* loving rather than to *make* love happen.

Sweet Timothy
— for Jane on our 25th

I
(1970-72)

White are the beds of April,
waylaid beautiful fire
burning out of luck and life,
being earlier than I have ever thought,
where, once leaves breathe
in the walk of morning,
light flakes green.

Children are the first awake,
before milk or bird,
waiting for sound
and the secret bowers of summer.
Wind through sunlight.
Cobwebs on the rhubarb leaves.
What flows between me but
even spring,
even water
drying inward from the edges.

Sweet timothy of days and my dear
tell me many times
how hot are the beds of summer.

Say at last a bush is burning,
lovely as life
when the thought is on us,
hatched in loitering acts
and rising all the time,
though there is time enough
to die in life as lovely as aching;
or being found out in my prayer,
leave me half on fire,
throwing off attitudes like flame,
for these grave eyes divine what
but that there is not in being one
I may love after you.

II
(1994)

These uncertain hands
carry both love and poison,
have been our undoing many times,
but refuse to disappear.
Take them again—
recall their stubborn particulars
as we return to the bluegreen meadow
wholly dependent on our inabilities.
Goldfinch, redwing, the hawk-stunned air,
the endlessly uttering grasses
say still there breathes no other
across a thousand miles of evening.

Part VIII

AN ENDLESS VOW

21

LIVING STARDUST

Thoughts of good can be among the most corrupting influences in life. I say this both to keep the cynics from despairing and as a warning. Fear and helplessness are real experiences. It is too easy to ignore the intrinsic duality of goodness by thinking we *are* good, or that we grasp the essence of goodness—which of course instantly, if unwittingly, drives us in the other direction.

How often do you hunker down into the hole in your heart in fear of the threat of the world, the threat of everything—of sin, of violence, of loss and grief, of damnation, of pain? Even in the valley deep with belief, voices ring with doubt. When you sit in meditation and watch yourself follow your breath, that scrutiny separates you from your breath. Can you ever return over that distance? As post-modern individuals, perhaps we expect nothing but want it all. W. S. Merwin notes in "A Claim": "Expecting nothing, caught by what was never there . . ." and in "That Music": "one more in the long trailing / troops of figures that had been believed but / had never existed . . . no singing among the stars . . . no ringing single note threaded the great absences . . . no echoing of space in space . . . not in the choiring of water . . . not . . . living through the thrush of dusk or the wren of morning."

It is all too much. It's not that the center cannot hold but that there is no center. Who's in charge? Where's the structure, the order, the meaning? Since World War II these questions have been asked so often they take on the quality of existential platitudes.

One of my sisters teaches school in the foothills of the Smokey Mountains in North Carolina. She is a special education teacher and her students actually fit the stereotype of children who are victims of rural inbreeding and neglect. These are children, she is quick to remind people, including her superiors, not a joke. Their lives are real, confused, burdened with disabilities over which they have no control. These children are society's throwaways. In the past, they would have been institutionalized or left at home to lives of abuse we cannot even imagine. My sister weeps as she talks about them, about how she loves them, about how the state of North Carolina makes her job almost impossible with paperwork designed to cover the butts of the bureaucrats who run the system. Most of the students are junior-high age, facing the normal insanity of the onset of puberty without the normal tools or capacities to handle it. She was required to introduce them to algebra.

"Mrs. Johnson, we can't do that."

"Oh, yes you can!"

"No we can't. We're too stupid."

"No you're not. I'll show you!"

And she had these kids, labeled by the system as barely educable, doing a conga line along the floor of the trailer, to which their classroom has been exiled, chanting a rap-song of numbers as they stepped back and forth across the figures she had drawn on either side of a line on the floor. By the end of the day they knew how to balance equations. .

On her birthday she walked into class to a wild chorus of "Happy Birthday!" and "How old are you, Mrs. Johnson?" She's just turning fifty, though she doesn't look it, but she said:

"I'm way over sixty!"

"Wow!" they said.

Then one boy, I'll call him Robbie, came up to her and scrutinized her face and eyes.

"Damn, Mrs. Johnson, if it weren't for that zit on your nose, you wouldn't look a day over forty."

Robbie wore a back brace because of a combination of an "accident" at home and a congenitally weak lower back. At one point later in the morning, Robbie was drifting across the classroom and my sister walked up behind him and tapped the brace.

"Anybody home?" she asked.

Robbie turned to her with a puzzled look and thought for a long moment.

"Why no, Mrs. Johnson, I'm here!"

She loves this open innocence. She will not let anyone throw away any of them. She does not, as many adults do, blame them for being as they are. They seem to know this and respect her for it. And they know it's a bad idea to "get her Irish up," as they are fond of calling her temper. She's no fool with them. She has no misty vision of some miracle bringing them to the full life other children have. She hasn't much time for useless hope or idealism. But she has time to love them unreservedly. No one else will. No child deserves not to be loved. No child deserves to be discarded however much their needs demand of us.

Large and small, the demons are around us. The owl of death haunts our dreams. Lying in bed on a grey winter morning, for a passing instant we can't remember what we look like or what names attach to us. My beloveds, you are living stardust and even your thieving delusions cannot take that from you.

22

ARRIVING IN THE IRRELIGIOUS DARK

Praise is how you are in the world. It depends upon nothing and has no object. It is very exact and exacting. We will use irony and detachment as a stay against what love requires. But to what possible end but our own loneliness? Unconditional praise is what love requires. It is not waving hands in the air, nor singing hallelujah, nor bowing in worship of something other. It is getting out of bed in the morning and it is *how* you get out of bed in the morning. It is putting your feet on cold floorboards, with an urgency to get to the bathroom, recognizing with Master Dogen that "not a thing in the entire universe is missing from the present time." It is an intimacy with this very moment, this present time.

I hear a voice out there saying, "Oh, sure, I always get out of bed thinking of Master Dogen before I take a leak." That is not what I mean at all. I mean experiencing the timelessness and totality of the moment is nothing special. Usually we are aware only of the irreversibility of processes, including our lives, and our separate place along the flight of the arrow of time. "Hey, I'm the one who's dying here." Oh? Sometimes a small thing will shift our perception so the directional paradigm vanishes. We claim it again quickly, but know something has changed.

I'm on my way to school, a walk of a little under a mile. I'm in third grade. I hate school, but it's morning in October and I am not really thinking about school. I start to skip. The sidewalk goes slightly downhill and rises crazily over tree roots in places. I begin to run. I can run very fast, faster than anyone of any age in my school. I love to run. My feet feel light. I am running as fast as I ever have. I stop feeling my feet or my legs. I think this is what flying must be like. Today we would say the endorphins had kicked in, but I am just happy, beyond happy, running, running totally. The world flashes by and at the same time everything moves in slow motion, my steps are so perfect and precise that I feel faster than time itself. In school I spend the rest of the day staring out the window at myself running.

On another day I am walking home. On the other side of the street under some huge evergreens the sidewalk runs three feet higher than this side. I cross over the quiet street. It is a vast cliff. I climb among the roots of the trees, poised at the edge of oblivion. My home is miles, countries away. The struggle over the terrain is so difficult I can think of nothing else. My hands are raw from climbing and my shoes beaten from stones and roots. I look up and there is my mother bearing down on me. Where have I been? Didn't I know it was supper time? Where did the time go?

One of my sisters had a high school friend who was born blind. Her perception of the world was so radically different from what we took for granted, including her attitude toward what we called sight (she could not regret what she could not know), that having her around was always surprising. She, Susan, visited us once when we lived in Puerto Rico. With her, we became more aware of the air, the smells, the particularity of thousands of sounds.

One evening the three of us got it into our heads to visit El Moro, the old fort guarding the harbor of San Juan. Susan's delight in the echoing corridors and the cobbled courts made us all feel like children let loose. We ran about laughing and shouting to one another. On one of the lookouts with a pepperpot tower, Susan climbed up on the wall and bet us she could walk around the outside. My knees turned to water. It was at least one hundred feet to the rocks and the sea below. But she couldn't see that, she had no sense of distance or danger as it applied in this case. Before we could reply, she got up, grabbed the wall and shuffled her way entirely around the pepperpot. Just looking out the gun-slits was too much for me. I had to turn away and hope her grip did not falter. It didn't. Charged with this success, we scrambled over a wall into a cemetery full of, to us, exotic mausoleums. It was quite dark by now as we traipsed up and down the rows, making up stories about the garish structures.

Over the other wall of the cemetery was La Perla, the barrio at the foot of El Moro, one of the most famous barrios in the world, along with those in Calcutta and Rio. Music and cooking smells drifted over to us. Susan wanted to go there. Without thinking, we agreed and helped her over the wall. The three of us began walking the narrow ways. This was an insane act. No gringo ever went there at all, much less after dark, much less two attractive young women and a fairly innocuous guy. Even the local cops avoided the place. Everyone would say it was a death warrant and no one would find our bodies. At the very least, we'd be stripped of everything and left to die. None of these thoughts crossed our minds, arrogant with youth. My sister and I noticed how the smells reminded us of Africa, the slightly sick-sweet smell of palm smoke, the pong of human waste, local music, children everywhere, voices shouting, and boxes, wood-scraps, corrugated tin patched together to make dwellings and lean-tos of a community as poor as any in the world. Disease, violence, drugs, you name it, get their good name started in places like this. Hundreds died during hurricanes, swept away into the sea. The survivors always came back quickly to nest again.

Susan asked us to describe everything. We became absorbed in details we related to her. People watched us, shocked. Who were these white folks? Where did they come from (we'd sort of landed in the middle of things over the wall)? Were they stupid or what? People watched us to see who would make the first move on us. But a mystery was becoming attached to our unheard of presence. We never noticed. We talked with Susan, waved hello boldly to everyone. My sister, whose Spanish and local accent was good, spoke to children. Then we heard the whispers.

"¡Mira! ¡Mira! ¡Una Ciega! ¡Mira!" "Look, look, a blind girl! Look, she's come to visit us." In that instant everything went into that strange slow motion. We became aware of not just where we were walking but of the whole barrio whispering, of smiles, of curiosity, of tears for Susan's darkness, of gratitude that we in some way blessed them with a visit in this place no one visits, home of the world's throwaways. People wanted to touch her, hold her hand, ask for a blessing. "¡Mira! Gracias Ciega, muchas gracias."

We were suspended in a total present. So surprised, without fear or judgment, so grateful and open ourselves to see life looking out attentive and kind, blameless from dark eyes, eyes that could see, to one who could not, one who nevertheless saw what few have seen, the opening of the flower of gratitude in what custom had taught to be unfruitful ground. Space-time stopped. Being-time opened before us.

It is available to each of us at any moment at any time in life. What is it? Is it real?

When I was about ten, we lived for a brief time on Long Island. At that time, during the huge postwar Catholic revival of the 1950s, all the parochial schools in the town of Westbury were filled beyond capacity and I had to go to public schools. This meant I also had to go to catechism classes after school at our parish church a couple of times a week to make up for what I was missing in public school. Because it was considered a sin to miss the class and my dad had the car at work until late every night, I had to bike there through heavy suburban traffic, regardless of weather or how dark it was. My mother brooked no arguments. She never even thought there was a choice.

One day at class a Franciscan monk visited us. I had never seen a monk before, save in pictures of St. Francis in our daily missal. This man looked like he had just walked out of one of those pictures. As far as I knew the clergy dressed only in black or the bright vestments for mass. Here was a man in a coarse brown robe tied by a rough white cord, carrying a long walking stick, wearing sandals and sporting a tonsured head. I was utterly taken with his strange and somehow wonderful appearance. He told us he was on a pilgrimage walking from parish to parish to talk with young people just like ourselves. I can't recall anything else he said, but the sort of life he must lead fascinated me.

When the class was over I asked our nun what the monk did when he wasn't on pilgrimage. "Oh, he lives in a monastery."

"What is a monastery?" I had no idea what a monastery was.

"It's a place where monks live, mostly in silence."

"What does he do so quietly in a monastery?"

Trying to keep it simple and to shut me up, she said, "He talks to God all day."

Wow, I thought, *what could be cooler than that! Talking to the Big Guy all the time. No need to talk to scary parents, schoolteachers, boring friends, or anyone else, except the Maker of Everything!*

When I got home that evening I told my mother I wanted to be a monk. In those days you could enter seminary at age twelve, or so I remember. "That's nice dear," she said, "Why don't you wait awhile, meet some girls, and then see what you think." So I did that. I traveled the world, met girls, married one, had a life and children, messed things up pretty badly, and then, forty-five years later, I did become a monk, just not a Catholic one.

The truth is not sequential. Nor is God. There is no one waiting at the gates with his buddies, Peter and Michael, when we finally come to the end of the road. Our linear, directional hopefulness is just a desire for wish-fulfillment, the self-deceptive wish that the Divine is somehow modeled on our needs and within our experience of time and life, and that we, personally, matter to it. Hope has ever masked the optimist's disappointment with experience. The Dharma, the all-inclusive truth beyond dualities of real and unreal, without beginning or end, is not sequential.

The moment I understood this my life changed. It was a clear, wintry day in February or March and I was sitting in Russ Blackwood's

prestigious Eastern religions class. The class met in the science building for some reason and looked out over woods and the back of the old
hockey rink. Professor Blackwood, a tall, lean man and self-proclaimed
"American Pragmatist" (which he left completely unexplained) was sitting in the lotus posture on top of his desk, guiding a debate on the
nature of God. I was a junior in college.

Somehow I had cajoled and badgered my way into the class, collaring
Russ and my advisor whenever I'd meet them in the halls, begging to
be allowed in. I had not done well in the prerequisite history of philosophy course, especially in the section on Aristotelian logic. Russ had his
doubts but eventually relented. It was a wonderful class, one in which I
did not so much learn as soak up everything in sight. The debate about
the nature of God had been going on for a while. We had read some
Sufi text and by this time, late in the section, Catholics, Jews, atheists,
and spiritual drug-heads (like myself) had settled into fairly rigid and
predictable positions regarding God. Suddenly Jim Iritani (I am sure
he doesn't remember this), an artist, piped up with, "But God is not
sequential!"

I froze. I stopped listening to anything else. I do not know what
karmic circumstances had brought me to that moment of vulnerable
openness, but those words rang in me like a deep bell. Indeed they
still ring there. The debate continued, with Russ asking Jim to carry
the thought further, but I have no recollection of the rest of it. I knew
absolutely with my very bones that what Jim had said was true, true in
a way I had not understood true before. I did not realize it then, but in
that moment my path turned decidedly and I began making my slow
painful way to the Buddhist priesthood. It was a statement perhaps
tossed off, and while I knew it to be true I did not know what it meant.

This was what was different about this truth, that I knew its truth
without understanding it. It made no difference that it was without
sensible or logical referents. It threw into relief all my questions about
faith, time, meaning. It is a statement that shoves all our faces into the
final extremity of death, for do we not look at death as the end of our

linear lives? For many years I'd lost touch with this experience, but I did not lose some essential residue that remained in my heart. It came back to life, like a seed long dormant that encounters the right conditions at last, like a solution over-dense with dissolved matter.

Many things contributed to the ripeness of the moment, my family, my Zen practice, but the crystal that clarified the supersaturated solution my life had become arrived in the person of someone dead several years before I came to Zen. I never knew Soen Nakagawa Roshi. Many have written about him and the wonder he brought to their lives. But I *feel* like I know him, often feel he is near, as I used to think of my guardian angel watching over my shoulder. No doubt this is partly romantic nostalgia for proximity to a legendary figure. It is also more. Like it or not, I am part of the Dai Bosatsu Mandala he articulated many years ago. He was teacher to both my teachers. Eido Roshi is his Dharma heir and Shinge Roshi is Eido Roshi's heir. Maurine Stuart— who, when Soen Roshi told her in private, as his student, she should call herself Roshi, became the focus of so much controversy—gave me the Precepts. Even my first publisher, Charles Tuttle, published Nyogen Senzaki's first major book, *The Iron Flute*. Nyogen Senzaki was Soen Roshi's lifelong friend, the person to whom Soen conveyed his vision of the Mandala, and the major reason he and Eido Roshi came to the West.

But there is more. Every time I attend sesshin at Dai Bosatsu, I make a small pilgrimage on the first night to the Sangha Meadow where a portion of Soen's ashes are laid. I make three profound bows, often in the dark and in snow half way up my thighs—just me, the deer, the snow—and humbly ask for his support in the forthcoming sesshin. Now, I don't normally do things like this. I gave up believing in ghosts and spirits, spooky or sacred, in my early teens. In AA meetings I get the heebie-jeebies when people say one should pray to God and *ask* to be given things, from sobriety and peace of mind to better jobs. To me that isn't praying, it's begging of the most demeaning, self-centered sort. My first sesshin, Rohatsu, I'd heard there was a marker for Soen in the Sangha Meadow, so I went, curious to see something connected with this Zen master whom everyone said was one of the great T'ang Dynasty crazy Zen heroes returned. Ice was cracking in the trees. The flat toned wind chimes sounded plaintive in the late November dark. Suddenly I found myself on the ground bowing and talking to him as though I had indeed been his student.

Some years later Eido Roshi told the story of his mala beads, a kind of rosary used, among other things, to count repetitions of sutras in chanting, and his own experience on Dai Bosatsu mountain in Japan. Soen Roshi used to spend long retreats there and it is where he created the dharani of *Namu Dai Bosa*. Eido Roshi was always a bit skeptical about that dharani. It wasn't part of the main tradition of Rinzai Zen, nor was he all that certain about the efficacy of chanting it over and over, though he did so in honor of his teacher. While visiting the mountain and chanting the dharani, he rubbed the beads given to him by Soen Roshi together as part of the ritual. They burst apart, something that had never happened to him before. He was filled with a sense of Soen Roshi's presence and the interconnectedness of the Dai Bosatsu Mandala begun on this mountain where he was kneeling. He took this as a sign and later shared the beads with his own sangha at Dai Bosatsu Zendo. I now wear one around my neck and so maintain this daily connection through one of my teachers with Soen Nakagawa, a man I have never met but have somehow come to cherish as though I had. A religiously inclined friend said, upon hearing this story, that Soen was my real teacher reaching me through these others. That, of course, is how Dharma transmission works. Past, present, future have no meaning in this context.

Certainly he was an appealing figure. Two anecdotes will suffice, perhaps. In his introduction to *Endless Vow: The Zen Path of Soen Nakagawa*, Eido Roshi writes:

> On another occasion he asked me, "Tai-san (as Eido Roshi was then known), what do you think about Nietzche's 'God is

dead?'" This was so unexpected that I was speechless. So Soen Roshi answered, "God is not dead, since he was never born."

Soen Roshi was famous for throwing convention out the window. This had enormous appeal to freewheeling Americans, but it often appeared rude or insensitive to Japanese compatriots. His breaks with the expected were always purposeful, however. Shinge Roshi tells how she went to her first dokusan with him:

My turn came. Feeling entirely unworthy of Soen Roshi's time, I timidly struck the bell and walked up the stairs. I entered the dokusan room, but Soen Roshi's cushion was empty. Then I saw him standing near the door, as though to pounce on me. "Come," he said. My mind raced. He had seen right through me! I wasn't going to be allowed to have dokusan! He led me back down the stairs and stopped at the landing. As I was forlornly about to continue down, he said, "Wait! Come here." He was standing at the window. I went over to him, and he gently positioned me so that I was looking out. There was the enormous, deep-red ball of the sun bursting over the horizon! I had passed right by it on my way to see Roshi, thinking that dokusan had to take place in the dokusan room.

The connectivity I have experienced through Shinge Roshi and Eido Roshi took me a long time to accept. It is the transmission of mind directly from teacher to student, from teacher to student, endlessly, from generation to generation. There is no loss of content or degradation of quality because it remains direct, clear. Behind Shinge I hear Eido. Behind Eido I hear Soen. Behind Soen I hear Gempo—on and on. How can this be? I do not know. My western training refuses to accept the literal reincarnative connotations. It is not the Voice of God. It is not really a long string stretching into the past, though that is a common way to describe it. It is immediate, here already—waiting for me, the idiot grandson unable to open his eyes.

Beecher Lake, the highest lake in the Catskills at three-thousand feet, rests at the foot of Dai Bosatsu Mountain, the New York State edition. It is rich with life—beaver, fish, fowl, and smaller beings, including salamanders or newts. One afternoon during Holy Days sesshin, I was sitting in the sun on the terrace of Dai Bosatsu Zendo. That morning I had passed an extraordinarily difficult koan and now it was lunch break time. I was joyous, exhausted, drained in every way. It was April and there was still snow banked around the grounds and terrace, but I was in a sunny spot and the sun toasted the slate and my weary body.

I found myself looking at something right next to my hand, which was resting on the warm stone. It took me several minutes to register what I was seeing. How could this be, perhaps two hundred yards from the lake at the end of winter? There was still ice-skim on the north-facing edge of the lake. What I was seeing was the tiny, perfectly formed body of a newt. I realized it was dead and had been so a long time. It was dried out, more like an empty paper shell, yet perfectly formed and intact, lighter than a leaf. Gently I picked it up and spent a few minutes examining it. How could it be here? An inch to the left and I would have sat on it, crunched it to dust without knowing it was there.

My eyes looked up through the trees under the bright April sky, across the lake to the Sangha Meadow. It seemed a priceless gift, this small dead thing. It was like a key that unlocked a door in my sense of self. For a moment that self dropped away, a moment like sublimation.

SOEN'S DRAGON

There are some things we know
before we had words to tell us
we knew them.
We are fastened to them
though they are not fastened to us.

Remember once April hills held the snow
and field stones were warm in the sun.
I basked like an old dog
and found a newt dead by my foot.
It's with me now.
The eye sockets are empty.
There is nothing inside.

How did the body survive the winter?
How did it escape
the birds and small animals
to die there,
dry, perfect in each detail,
whole down to the last brown toe?

As we clutch and breathe
the smoke of sublimation
I hold this light of emptiness
in my hand.

It is part of our tradition to write a poem when one is to be ordained. I found myself in awe of the step I was taking, fearful of the commitment and responsibility, knowing that somehow I had also passed the point of choice and was entering upon one of the inevitabilities of my life. Just before I was ordained, Shinge Roshi gave me prepublication excerpts from what became *Endless Vow*, upon which she was then working with Eido Roshi and Kaz Tanahashi. The opening lines in the excerpt, titled "Upon Determining to Become a Monk" were:

> Reflecting my heart
> sky and water
> sobering chill.

I felt a chill run down my own back. I knew that taking this step was not trivial.

I had always thought masters did inevitable things without the usual trepidation. Infinite responsibility was a scary prospect. Later, when *Endless Vow* was published, the title of the excerpt had become "A Monk's Determination" and the translation changed somewhat to:

> Clearness!
> sky and water
> reflecting my heart.

This tells another part of Soen's story. It would be interesting to go into the nuances of translating Japanese to English and the differences in consciousness each language represents, but I am not the person to engage in that discussion. I would never have seen the earlier, put aside version of the poem had it not been for my teacher. Eido Roshi has often pointed out that Soen did not become a monk in order to engage in a priestly administrative career. Soen was completely surprised when Gempo Roshi, his teacher, made him abbot of Ryutakuji.

I left my own church and the possibilities of becoming a monk there only in part because of its appalling history of war, brutality, cruelty, mendacity, betrayal, corruption, and death. I wanted a way in which I could "talk to God all day," a nonsequential God who was closer to me than I was to myself—already and always discovering. Soen Roshi identified himself with Bassui, who asked the question, "Who is it who hears the sound?" Who is it who takes these steps in the yellow dust of the world? Soen Roshi answers:

Crawling out from the Dead Sea
spring glitters
over my body

I heard Eiso Roshi tell the following story during a lecture he gave at my university during the 1993 centennial celebration of Buddhism in America we hosted. He recounts it again in *Endless Vow*. It is a quintessential Soen story, bringing East and West together seamlessly, filled with passion and skillful means, that deep sensitivity to the moment, what Eido Roshi calls *ichigo ichie*, an unrepeatable encounter. I quote in full from *Endless Vow*:

When I was Soen Roshi's attendant monk at Ryutaku-ji, there was an American professor who came to practice there. He was desperate to have some kind of insight experience. Evidently the koan Mu had been assigned to him, without any kind of explanation.

Many months passed and he was very frustrated. One day it happened that Soen Roshi invited him and me to his mother's hut to hear music and receive ceremonial tea. Roshi said, "Be seated." We sat down. The professor's mind was occupied with the koan he had been assigned. He asked, "Tell me, Roshi, how can I expedite my understanding of

Mu? What is the most effective way to practice Mu and get self-realization?"

Continuing to make the ceremonial tea, Soen Roshi asked him, "What did Jesus Christ say on the cross?"

The professor replied, "Well, he said, 'My God, my God, why have you forsaken me?'"

Soen Roshi said nothing and served the ceremonial tea, as if the conversation was over. But from the professor's point of view, it was not. So he asked again, "I came all the way from America; I want to know my true nature. So what is the most effective way to practice Mu?"

Roshi said, "Tell me, what did Jesus Christ say on the cross?" The professor replied again, rather impatiently, "'My God, my God, why have you forsaken me!'"

"No!" Roshi answered loudly. "Well, then, what *did* he say?" the professor asked in exasperation.

At that Soen Roshi stood up, spread his arms, became Jesus Christ, and cried in anguish, "My God, my God, why have you forsaken me?"

It is what Eido Roshi calls "direct, no explanation Zen."

Two of Soen's poems capture his essence for me, one is his death poem, reminding me so much of Maurine Stuart's last words, and the other is what I think of as his life poem, from which the title of the book about him comes, which echoes Setcho's famous line and yet remains freshly itself, as Soen Roshi did:

SPRING 1984—*Death Poem*

Mustard blossoms!
there is nothing left
to hurl away

And the life poem:

Bowing to Hakuin's Stupa at Ryutaku-ji in Mishima

Endless is my vow
under the azure sky
boundless autumn

I was about to write that my other teachers are still living, but that would not be quite correct. All my teachers are living right at this moment. How can this be? Am I making it up, a kind of metaphysical fiction to explain an inner experience?

No. It is real.

I did not think this relationship between teacher and student, this transmission of mind, was something for which we had a context in the West. But there is this, to me, startling movie by Alain Corneau, *Tous les Matins du Monde*, which came out and was a wild success in France though it fizzled in the United States—another kind of statement itself, I suppose. It purports to be the story of Marin Marais, court composer to Louis XIV, and his obscure teacher Sainte Columbe, about whom little is really known. Frankly, it doesn't matter who it is about and the music is a joy all in itself. But the story has many Zen-like echoes without once alluding to anything Eastern.

The young Marais, seeking a teacher, is turned away several times to test, among other things, the seriousness of his purpose before he is accepted by Sainte Columbe. There is tragedy and pain in the story, and a love interest, of course. Marais abandons his teacher, achieves great success at court, yet finds himself always turning back to a "something" he did not quite get, that mere talent could not bring him. In middle age he finds himself sneaking back to his master's house to listen to the master practice, in the hope of gleaning the master's secret. There is a climactic scene that always leaves me in a total meltdown of emotion—

because it is exactly the experience I have found with my teachers, with Shinge Roshi, with Eido Roshi, and in this newly apprehended manner, with my Dharma grandfather, Soen Roshi. The sequence begins with the words: "Each day dawns but once. . . " Why, in other words, do we wait?!

On a frozen night the fat and overdressed Marin Marais rides from court and sits shivering outside Sainte Columbe's practice hut. He hears the master shuffling about, playing some notes, talking to himself, longing for someone who really understands music as he does, so he can die in peace. It is his longing to transmit, mind-to-mind, the Dharma through music. Marais knocks and Sainte Columbe, old and grey and simply dressed, asks him what he seeks in music. "I seek sorrows and tears." He is allowed to enter. What follows is like a *mondo* (Zen dialogue) out of classic dokusan.

Marais says, "May I beg for one last lesson?"

Sainte Columbe replies with, "May I attempt the first lesson?"

He continues, "Music exists to express what words cannot say. What is it to you?"

Marais begins a litany of wrong answers, the rational struggle to conceptualize, to get it. It is a small leap to transpose *Dharma* for *music* in this conversation without changing any of its intent.

"God?" "No, God can speak."

"The ear?" "No."

"Gold? Glory? Silence?" "No."

"Other musicians? Love?" "No."

"Sorrows? Abandonment?" "No."

"Water offered to the Invisible?" "Close, but no."

Marais pauses a long time. "I don't know any more . . ."

A longer pause and then it comes out, softly, almost unbidden, "For the time before we were born, before we saw light, before we breathed."

Their hands clasp and they both know the other knows this is the truth. By giving up, letting go of the striving for discovery, teacher and student brought forth the answer that is already and always there. The teacher cannot make you get it, can only assiduously model the practice with his or her particular voice, for, as we often chant, whether singing or dancing, we are the voice of the Dharma. Only when the student stops struggling and grasping to match the teacher and realizes there is nothing to learn or be taught do all the doors and windows fly open and we are affirmed by all things blowing through us and through our teacher, for now there is no distance at all. Like radio waves, we don't see or hear anything unless we are tuned in. Without the proper instrumentation of the practice we cannot even know what is there. When we are tuned in it comes to us complete and it cannot be used up or diminished. We get the whole experience.

On Becoming a Monk

No one behind. No one ahead.
Just this place and point.
All escape routes end here
and the maps proved useless long ago.
The thousand disguises are in tatters
along the road behind.
Out here, vast emptiness—
the life-cries of the world's lost billions.

Just these guides
in the containing silence:
a thrush at dusk, a star at dawn.

Who puts his foot down again in the dust?
Whose foot again and again, ceaselessly?

When I can put my driven, grasping ego away for a while I join with my teachers to give them my gratitude. It is significant to me that Soen Roshi wrote his life poem while bowing to his great Dharma ancestor. I bow again to all my teachers:

BOWING
—*for Shinge Roshi and the sangha of Hoen-ji*

In this empty house
I have thrown
all the windows open for you.
Upstairs in the irreligious dark
nothing remains
to whisper as you approach.
Come, play here now,
each in your shimmering exactitude—
spring rains, flowering lilacs,
countless birdsongs.

23

FLOCKS OF FINCHES AT DAWN

We all know that if a cup falls from the table and breaks, no amount of wishing will reverse the process and send it back up to the table in one piece again. This is the arrow of space-time as we usually experience it. Dogen Zenji (thirteenth-century Japanese philosopher and Zen master who founded the Soto tradition), however, wrote about time, *uji*, or being-time. "If you believe that time only passes, you have not understood that time never arrives, never leaves." "Although understanding itself is time, understanding does not depend on its own arrival." "Being-time . . . means that time is always being, that all that *is* is time." Dogen also says that to study the true nature of the universe (to study the Way) is to study the self; to study the self is to forget the self; to forget the self is to be affirmed by all things.

One day late in October I was in the park near the university having my sandwich for lunch. It was a warmish spell after a killing frost. Most, but not all, of the plants and leaves were gone. I'd heard an old song by the group Kansas, coming from a dorm window, "Dust in the Wind (All we are is dust in the wind)," and found the lyrics running through my head, one of Eido Roshi's so-called "Dharma coincidences." After eating, I sat on a rock. I was, for some reason, acutely aware of the smells of October, the soil, leaves, air. I poked at the dirt with a twig. Suddenly, while still there with the twig I was also four years old playing in the dirt, not just remembering but actually in the place at Poole's

Corner outside of Doylestown, Pennsylvania. That October and this were fused instantly and opened to one another. I knew then that nothing disappears, not sound, not events, not moments.

Things change but the universe remains complete. All that is from all that was, all that will be from all that is. How can anything be excluded? It was neither a wrinkle in time nor some deeply felt nostalgia trip I experienced, but being-time of this being suddenly open. Neither here nor there, no thoughts nor conditions. Each thing around me affirmed the being-event most intimately in the living now, where there is no point or moment, where no one is home, because *place* and *home* no longer have meaning.

When everything is wonder-full there is no single thing, a thing apart from oneself to wonder about. The action of being does not take place in time, but in this momentless moment. Garry Wills cites the *Confessions* of St. Augustine, which he calls *The Testimony*:

> If we could suppose some particle of time which could not be divided into smaller particles, that alone deserves to be called the present, yet it is snatched from the future and flits into the past without any slightest time of its own—if it lasted, it could be divided into part future and part past. So there is no *present* as such.

Wills goes on to summarize the rest of this line of thought:

> And yet, paradoxically, we know the past only as a *present* memory and the future only as a *present* anticipation. There is, then, no real present and nothing *but* a real present. The mind brokers this odd interplay of times in a no-time.

Trust it. It is how you are in the world, your act of praise. You have no choice. This is the lesson of addiction and the lesson of being.

Where is the you, *when* is the you, *who* is the you when the point of identity is already gone? There are no exceptions. No one is better than this. No one is. To whom had I to prove someone—me—was? I thought my poems made something true in spite of me, that art and knowing were the same, that art made knowing and talking to God possible. But the God was *my* God . . . me.

There is nothing to prove and no one to whom it can be proven. No praise, nothing to praise, no one to do the praising. What kind of world is this? It is letting go of the fantasy life of self and an absolute. It is freedom from dependency on other, any kind of other. Praise is how you are in the world. Do I wrestle with my nostalgia for a private reality, some home of my own? Is anyone home? Why, no. Mrs. Johnson, I'm here? Real praise is being unconditionally. When you realize you are the light itself, it is not a *you* who is the light, but the light itself is the light.

I let my faithless breaths go. This nobody breathes your breaths, my beloveds. What is my vow? However innumerable the everyones and everythings, the no ones and nobodies, I vow my life—no blame, be kind, love everything—always.

Nothing to Prove

Who sees me by form,
who seeks me in sound,
wrongly turned
are his footsteps on the Way.
—Diamond Sutra, verse 26

We come to spring
both the stakes and the gambler,
putting our lives on the table
as if life were ours.
The light of suspicion in our eyes
recalls our own faithless breaths.
Swayed by words
we wander the wind
bewildered, looking for evidence
of something not quite there,
a face—proof we are not alone.
You are not alone my beloveds.
You cannot be alone.
There is no such thing as alone.
You are the air I breathe
and I am your very breath.
Because of you
I cannot be sad in this world.
And what with breakdowns and so on
who would say it hasn't been hard going?

Do you look up at Death there
by the roadside
jingling chips of your fate
in his pockets,
watching us under the cutting north wind,
the brilliant moon, the wild white clouds,
not so much there as beside the point?
And if you ask whether I regret starting out
my voice rises like flocks of finches at dawn
and blows across the deep blue sky.

AFTERWORD

When we first looked at this old farmstead in West Cork, now our home in Ireland, we were told that somewhere "down there" on a narrow strip of the property that fell steeply away was an orchard. A footpath went part-way down and then disappeared into an impenetrable tangle of six-foot-tall bracken, dense twisted bramble with canes more than an inch thick that ran even higher than the bracken, and countless unidentifiable weeds, saplings, and rampant grasses—all of which filled a secluded area in which one *might* imagine a small orchard. On one side rose a sheer, solid stone escarpment topped by an even denser growth of ancient gorse, so thorny and rough that it defied assault like a castle wall. On the other side were a stone wall and the sagging barns of Willie's farm, abandoned, sinking into boggy fields behind an overgrown hedgerow of hawthorn, ash, masses of wild ivy, pines, elder, and oaks. The whole place was also sinking into a jungle of weeds, rushes, and choking vines. There were no signs of the branches of fruit trees above the small sea of weedy neglect on the patch before us. An orchard? No way.

One mild sunny day during our first winter here, having invested in a heavy-duty strimmer, or weed-whacker, with a blade attachment, I decided to attack the jungle and see if I could discover this orchard. I was armored in tall green wellies, thick leather garden gloves, iron Carhartt overalls, a padded Carhartt vest over them, ear muffs to guard against the powerful whine of the strimmer, and a meshed mask to keep flying debris away from my face and eyes. I really felt like an armored knight going to some strange battle, the outcome of which was far from certain.

And a battle it was. It took me more than three days to clear an area roughly the size a tennis court. From the broad ruthless sweeps of the strimmer I was covered from head to foot in a green surface of shredded leaf, twig, sappy moisture, and bits of seed, along with a settling cloud of dust and debris. After just a couple of hours my arms began to feel like rubber from the weight of the machine, which sent numbing vibrations through my hands. My wife began gathering the masses of fallen debris to create a bonfire with the express glee of an avowed pyromaniac. We were getting there, but it was very hard work.

Gradually some small trees did begin to emerge, bent and twisted, almost falling over from the weight of the huge choking brambles. I began to take more care in my cutting, hoping to avoid scarring the bark of the struggling plants. In the end, exhausted but happy, we looked upon six apple trees, a pear tree, and what turned out to be two plum trees, all still alive. At that moment of weary but joyous revelation, we couldn't be absolutely sure what each tree was, save that they were fruit trees, given their unpruned, gnarled state of neglect. We had to wait until the following summer to see what they were and what, if anything, they produced.

The pear tree produced one pear. One. The plums produced nothing at all. But the apples seemed to burst with fruit in the joy of finally being free in the wind and the sun. Only one did we know right away, the Bramley. Huge green, lumpy cooking apples, so rich in crisp sour tanginess that they make Granny Smiths look like bland afterthoughts. The five other trees were at least three varieties and we are still trying to discover what types they are. We are learning to tend them, how and when to prune, when to let them alone, when to pick the fruit, and how to maintain the space so the trees can grow completely into themselves. We have found our orchard.

Now there is a story of another kind of orchard that was lost in a jungle of thorns and neglect, where the fruit bearing beings became bent and twisted from the weight of fear, death, error, and ignorance; a story that gives us a glimpse of the hard work of cutting away the tangled brambles that choked heart and soul. My wife and I both had to armor ourselves, forge new weapons and tools, and enter another kind of strange battle, the outcome of which was also far from certain.

Time passes. If you are still enough, you can hear the dew grazed air stirring down the many streets and roads your feet have taken you, you can hear the stars falling. When you look back you can see the nights you have lived moving in a blur of shadow, so that one cannot be told from another. And the daylight of your eyes sees a crowded blur of events and people turning and touching one another, but in what order and with what interconnecting influence, it is all too much to make out. Twelve years in a flash. Twelve years in a long muddle of hurt, failure, insight, and joy. Time passes. The universe is breathing.

This book was originally published in 2001 under the title *St. Nadie in Winter: Zen Encounters with Loneliness.* It had a modest success and was reasonably well reviewed. The publisher at the time, however, was being absorbed into a larger multinational and underwent a change of direction soon after publication. When the contract period ended, they let the book go out of print. Since then *St. Nadie* has taken on a life of its own on the internet, especially among the lost and lonely "seekers" of the Way. But it also lives on among therapists, who have created a still ongoing conversation about it in blogs and other social media.

When I approached Wisdom Publications about the possibility of publishing a new edition, they agreed to pursue it. Yet it couldn't just be thrown out there again. We thought to reorganize it a little, making the story flow more easily and collecting the bulk of the poems at the end. The poems had been the initial motivation behind *St. Nadie* and it is still important to read them. It is also important to say something about the years since 2001. That is the other story, though here I will tell it in brief because there are already enough true confessions in *St. Nadie.*

My life in the years between *St. Nadie*'s first publication and this one became a very troubled life once again, but, in the end, it has opened into something completely new and unexpected. As I put the original book behind me I found I was putting other, valuable things behind me too. Having completed the book gave me a sense of arrival. I think that was a mistake. I was changed, but I did not know in what way. What happened to that life I had found and tended for so long?

In the more than a dozen years since the first edition of this book was published, I have had three life-changing experiences that have confirmed for me the knowledge that despite mendacity, pain, disease, and unnecessary death in the world, life can be good. The first was a death sentence—I was told that, if I were lucky, I would have five years to live. The second was a relapse into addiction after twelve years of sobriety. The relapse was in part a response to the death sentence, and it was a deeper, far worse, and more difficult-to-emerge-from collapse than the first, which I have already described in the pages of this book. It took me five grim years to crawl out of that hole, but when I did, what opened before me was the most creative period of my life. Feeling more deeply than ever that I wanted to live and grow old with my wife, I realized the deepest wish to return *home* to Ireland. Coming home, in more ways than one, coming home and what I found here, this is the third thing.

Graves' disease. It is a very serious hyperthyroid condition brought about by stress and overwork and it leads to the collapse of the auto-immune system. Graves' disease is rare in men, but it seems there is a genetic vulnerability to autoimmune problems in my family. If it isn't caught in time the disease can be fatal. Because the symptoms are so much like those of routine stress, mine went undiagnosed until specific elements of the later stages of the illness showed themselves. In my case I lost a tremendous amount of weight, which, before I knew what was happening, I thought was great. Who in midlife doesn't want to shed a few pounds? Then my eyes began to bulge out in a very dramatic, offputting, and uncomfortable way.

My overworking thyroid gland had to be stopped. Eventually, once my thyroid gland was shut down, I began to regain all the weight I had lost, and then a lot more. It was as though the air itself was fattening. Dieting made no difference whatsoever. My metabolism had changed. It appeared that the disease was in remission, but when there was a mix up with my medication, it returned with real virulence and affected my heart. I developed dilated cardiomyopathy—congestive heart failure. After the cardiologist explained what was happening to me, I asked what the prognosis was. I didn't want any soft-talk; I wanted the truth so I could face reality. He said simply that if I did all the right things and the medications worked, I might have five years to live. I was just over fifty years old. It was Christmas. I had to drive home alone in the snow and tell my family that I was dying.

Around the same time my wife was offered a major promotion in her career, something she had worked long and hard for many years to achieve. The promotion lifted her from the ranks of management to a directorship in a major multinational corporation, allowing her to break through the glass ceiling encountered by so many intelligent and creative women. It also meant we would have to move to Baltimore, Maryland, a five hour drive away from Syracuse, New York. Our children were already grown: our son was nearly finished with undergraduate work and our daughter was beginning her independent adult life in Chile.

As for myself, I was losing interest in what I was doing. I found that the exciting and challenging seminars that I had been delivering for seven years at the university, which looked at the history of ideas through the history of the book, had lost their magic for me. I had also become exhausted by my work as a Zen Buddhist priest. I was president of the board at the Zen Center, as well as master of ritual, and, though not by official title, I was called on to perform many of the responsibilities of head monk. Aside from my work at the Zen Center, I was meditation chaplain at a local rehab, an unpaid Buddhist chaplain at the university, and was not only on the board of the InterReligious Council of Central New York but also a member of its executive committee, which at that time was deeply involved in preventing the violence that was threatened in a local Native American (Iroquois) land claims issue. I was worn out.

I saw my wife's promotion as a good thing, as an opportunity for change. I had no personal reason to stay in Syracuse. I had reached the peak of my professional day job. I was having a book published by an international publisher. Things were looking good. Yes, definitely time for a change. And then I received my fatal health report. Suddenly I felt the weight of moving away from our home of eighteen years, of leaving all of our friends behind, of walking away from my spiritual and recovery support system, and from the work through which I had garnered respect in ways I had not experienced before. But I had supported my wife in her career throughout all of our lives together. I could hardly stop now.

My wife had to be at her assignment in November well before we would be ready to move our household there—as it turned out, the better part of a year because I had to go on disability from work with my heart condition. The frame of my days disappeared. I would be home alone with tasks I wasn't really allowed to be doing for obvious health reasons, but that nonetheless needed to be done. We had no one else to do them. So I set about taking care of things, thinking that the more "normal" I behaved the easier it would be to cope with my responsibilities and the growing realization of what was happening to me.

To my sad surprise, many of the people I had thought of as friends drifted away. Friends at the university continued with their work, but because I was no longer involved, they were no longer involved with me. Similarly, I found that those at the Zen Center were there for their practice and not for me. When I was no longer present there, I slipped out of their consciousness. Save for a small handful of people, no one came to see me; no one invited me out. Eventually, after half a year of house hunting, we completed the move in August.

Although the focus at that time should have been my wife, her new challenges, and our settling in, I gradually slipped into a mindset in which everything I experienced was about me and most of it was negative. In AA we are always told, "It's not all about you." But when you are dying it *is* all about you. Dying is something we all do, alone. How did I want to live my life now that there wasn't very much left of it? This is where the challenge to the maturity of one's Buddhist practice begins to show itself. My practice was clearly not very mature at all, despite the fact that I thought that I had everything under control; that I could rely on my training and experience to pull me through to my approaching end.

But I began drinking again. "After twelve years of sobriety," I thought, "I may as well go down laughing." I could do what I considered to be all my good-boy things, like packing and sorting and cleaning, and I could also take time out for a little lightness to ease the physical and metaphysical pain of my condition. I began to relapse.

Relapse is not how it is in films or books, where one sip of demon rum and you are back in the gutter. It takes time. It's like the first time round: start with a little, then a little more, and finally a lot more. At first you can hide it or explain it away, but eventually there is no denying that you can't stop. The difference with relapse was that the whole process happened faster than the half a lifetime it took to first fall into addiction, and the hole was much deeper and a whole lot harder to crawl out of. And when you relapse, all the catch phrases of recovery, all the steps, all the well-meaning words become fatuous. If they didn't work the first time, how could they work now? Eventually the voice of the disease begins to eclipse your own and you no longer know which speaks for your condition in the world. Now I was dying in another way too.

I couldn't see it, and perhaps I didn't really care, but I was heading to yet another crisis in my life. It became my "bottom." My wife's absorption in her work and her growing anger as I slid deeper into relapse made it difficult for me to say anything to her about just how alone and desperate I was feeling. I told myself neither she nor anyone else cared. I felt fat, ugly, bug-eyed, and unwanted. No one seemed to be looking beyond all that to a real me. In this depressed and desperate state, unable to control my drinking or how I behaved under its influence, I broke the trust of someone who looked up to me as a friend and mentor. For a variety of personal and ethical reasons I cannot say specifically what happened, only that it did.

Word of what had happened reached my teacher at the Zen Center. After that everything fell apart. I had broken trust and the heart of my vows—*do no harm*. I resigned from the Zen Center. I made clear to the members of the Zen Center, to my teachers, and to my family what had happened. I sincerely apologized to everyone, and was excoriated, as one might expect, by my teacher at the center. I honestly did not think I was capable of hurting as I had. Yes, I was ill and my illness had affected my behavior, but that did not excuse it. I did it.

It is often said in recovery programs that when an addict behaves irrationally, tries to justify his using or his actions, that it is his disease speaking. Research now shows that it is literally true when we look at the physiological, neurological and psychological changes, caused by the chemicals in the substance, that actually occur. In real terms the addict is not the person he once was. He really cannot see, feel, hear, or understand the nature of his actions save only as they serve his addiction. I could not, obviously, see this in myself at the time, but I did see it later when working with a severely anorexic patient. While she was talking quite normally as herself about her condition I saw her eyes change. Suddenly it was not her but her disease speaking, justifying her obsessions. This is a deep body and soul wound that is very difficult to heal. It cannot be done alone, no more than open heart surgery can be done by oneself.

I knew I couldn't undo the damage. How could I continue my practice as a Buddhist monk? Would a real monk do this? Was I just using the vulnerability of the needy for my own ends? The shame of these thoughts was crushing.

A senior monk at the monastery helped me a great deal when in response to my shame he simply asked, "What is a monk?" I have spent years looking for the answer to that question in my life. I kept my morning mediation rituals and the rituals of certain special days over the calendar year. I entered myself into an outpatient rehab. I really couldn't hack it and needed help—I could see that much. I also reached out to offer healing, or at least comfort, to others by sharing my own humanity and experiences at hospitals and rehabs. I gave free talks about Buddhism at Johns Hopkins School of Nursing and elsewhere. I was even the "Spiritual Director" at an annual AA retreat held at a Catholic seminary. My wife and I created a teahouse that served as a great retreat space for small groups of friends from AA.

That my wife and I needed counseling as a couple had become very clear. That we both wanted it and wanted to hold together what had become utterly brittle was a very good sign. Once, like many men, I thought of counseling as a sign of weakness, a sign that I was too soft in the head to make it on my own. But it became obvious to me, as I myself became an aid and counselor to people in the extremities of need, that such an attitude is stupid and wasteful. We take aspirin for headaches, pills for hearts, thyroids, diabetes, constipation, bladder infections. Why not have help for our bloody minds and souls? If you are full of fear and questions that your doctor cannot answer about your impending death, why shouldn't you ask for help? I couldn't cure my heart failure without help. Why should I be able to cure my addiction without help? It is a recognized disease like any other. Why should I not seek help to cure the damage caused by my illness? If we can't help one another we are lost.

I worked hard—almost relentlessly—at all of this. I had to burn out the dark matter of the crisis. I needed to clean out all my misconceptions of myself and of Buddhism and grace and kindness and love. I had to start over by giving away all that I knew. It was the strength of the discipline and meditation and the real knowledge I had gained through years of giving myself to the practice that stood me in good stead. It allowed me to be strong enough to heal, change, and begin to grow again.

It is said you will know your teacher when you need him. Well, you can also know little truths when you need to hear them. The other day, while driving along the coast road into our little village, I caught a snatch of a country song on the radio out of Cork City. The words I heard were, *Do lovers really fall that way / and stand together come what may?* I felt a catch in my throat. As sentimental songs sometimes do, it grasped in a few words something that is not at all sentimental but on which hangs the essence of something unexpectedly true. I have been searching for a way to express the foundation of the love my wife and I have for each other and it lies in my answer to the question in that song: Yes.

Although what I want to write here is the most intimate and the most important part of everything that I have limped through thus far, I cannot go into it in any detail. Of course my wife was part of my every day of the last dozen years, but she has earned her privacy. She suffered me. Friends would ask her why she stayed. I go back to that country song: *Do lovers really fall that way / and stand together come what may?* We did, somehow, fall *that way* so many years ago, and it was she who taught me how to *stand together come what may.*

She had her own serious health problems. Both of her parents had died. She retired from more than thirty-five years in the business world, losing the daily frame of work and immediate direction. None of the required adjustments were easy for her. We were both aging, the changes in our health were affecting us differently. Many of our old "issues" came to light again, but in ways that reflected our individual inner changes. With the help of our counselor, to whom we returned as a new serious crisis loomed, we decided we could only face our future together.

As the years had gone by I had given over much of the decision making to my wife; she made more money, was not wrestling with addiction, and had the decisive career. I recalled how, when we were first married, we did things together, made our choices and lived our lives together rather than in parallel worlds. I wanted to go back there and find that way of being together again. Our life in Maryland had run its course and I knew that it would be a good thing to start someplace new, without the stains and history of lives we no longer lived. For years we had visited family in Ireland and had nearly moved there in 1971. We had fallen in love with West Cork, a wonderful combination of mild Cornwall and the rugged Highlands, only smaller. We decided to sell up, unload, clean house, downsize, and finally move to Ireland. I am an Irish citizen and have always felt at home in Ireland. We both felt sure she would too.

That whole process was yet another test and renewal. Selling a house in a down market meant almost certainly taking a big loss. Getting rid of a lifetime of stuff, some of it very precious to us, as are such things to any family, was deeply wrenching. Buying a house in another country with different laws, not to mention a different economy, is not something to be done lightly. But we did those things at a stage in life when most people are looking to settle and take it easy at last after years of labor.

Among the many specialized tools we created to take on this last great unpredictable battle against the lost and almost invisible orchard of our lives were the following: we meditated each morning; after breakfast we would have what we jokingly called a staff meeting, going over the many tasks that absolutely had to be accomplished that day; then we would decide who had to do what; at lunch we would check in to see how we each were doing; at about four in the afternoon we would knock off and have tea—to take a breather, not talk about much at first, then do a final check. This little process saved us and reinforced our regained capacity to really listen to each other.

Now on an old farmstead, looking out over Dunmanus Bay to the low mountains of the Mizen and the wayward clouds of weather in the West, we still have our afternoon tea and still talk about the day gone by. But our talk does not deal with shipping companies, tax laws, contractors working at either house to get each ready for sale or moving in. It tends to be more about the garden, how work is going in the studio, what or whom we encountered on market day, the last storm, what our young dog or five cats did to cause havoc this time, what our children are up to in Japan or the U.K.

This is our life here at *Baile*—home. We have found our orchard. The bent and twisted little trees have been freed of their tangling burdens. They have blossomed and the first fruits are emerging. No matter how hard you work, not every dream in life comes true. But some do.

WAY OF HARMONY
(from *One Morning*, Part 4)

With my darling companion
we gather the verbs, the nouns,
the ragged sentences and dust,
dump them in the compost of forgotten hymns,
wipe our hands on our pants,
reach out to grab each other's hand
and sing the most beautiful note
in all the voices of the world.

February 27, 2014

Terrance Keenan
Baile, Kealties
Durrus, West Cork

SELECTED POEMS

I.

DEATH OF THE FATHERS

The titles for this group of poems are lines from an essay by Alastair Reid on the death of his father.

A Sweetness Appears and Prevails

The reason we bother
to get up in the morning
is because of everything;
is because there is another arithmetic
without internal sense
and we ache at the borders;
is because the grey music
of the first chickadee before dawn
in the hemlocks
is the grinding engines of the humpyard
carried on morning air;
is because we are afraid
and know everyone is afraid
and do not know
who will soothe our tears

nor how many tears
we will hold unshed.
You seem to be you
and I seem to be me.
My sorrows are no greater
than your sorrows.
Thou art beautiful,
o my loves,
as tears are.

Unravel All This Interim

There is almost always
sometimes an answer.
Each summer day the cabbage-white
lives forever
and has no use
for the center of anything.
As for the dried stones of winter—
he's been them all.

Voices in Your Understanding

After this sadness
there is another sadness
and it must be addressed
without mute
for it presses urgently
for utterance
the endlessness of our longing
to return once again
to where the body
is blue leaves of sky
torn by the wind.

Mumchance

It is not for understanding
nor clarity of meaning
I listen carefully to you,
late thrush
across the meadows.

No Talk of Dying Well

When are you not afraid,
o my loves?
Go there to be born
a swirl of dust,
shadows of wind,
traceless cloud life.

I Am Not Ready to Be Without

Once upon a time
once and for all went away
without a trace.
The drunk—his heart bewildered,
he has become my companion.
The flying bird—
pathless in the winter sky,
she has become my heart.

Your Miscellaneous Way

Occupying your own skin with joy,
I watch you
listen to yourself living,
discovering each day
how much less of everything
steadies you into being.

We Forgave Each Other at an Early Age

Not the path
overgrown with dead summer grasses,
not the chilled cedar swamp
not the imperfect strategies,
not the grief,
not the world —
two old hawks
high over the darkening fields.

Too Old to Unfurl the World

Step by step we task the ground.
Step by step we taste the ground.
The sound of a name
the name of a sound.
The request of the soul
is closer
than we are to ourselves.

The Whole Household Is Pending

Dishes rattle in the sink.
Cupboards slam and the smell of food
rises from floor to floor.
So, say, then, from the heart
that you are the perfect day
and in you dwells
the little ruined light
that does not fail.

Loathe to Leave You to Your Death

When you are no good,
when you are fodder,
when your ground is soiled,
when the precious child leaves you
without looking back,
when your truth is falsified
by terror and death,
when all doors are ashes

and all walls are deaf,
when your breath tastes like iron,
when you will never know a day
without some sort of aching,
you are beautiful
o my loves
as tears are,
comely as the first holy snow.

II.

THE ORPHANED DARK

The titles for these poems, which accompany selections from *The Twenty-One Lullabies of St. Nadie*, are from Blake's *Proverbs of Hell*.

HE WHOSE FACE GIVES NO LIGHT SHALL NEVER BECOME A STAR

Deep frost. Sun and moon
at once in the dawn.
Our utter impermanence.
Sudden bitterness
springing all unbidden
at a word
that we will fail again
to be human.

Birds
sleep in the throat.
Behind the ribs
it is a bare open country.
This empty vessel overflowing.

LULLABY OF THE DREAMCATCHER

Hush. Be still.
The road is gone.
Speech and truth sleep
and only your dream
stands against darkness close at
    hand.
It is the place of night
and of time,
darkness without shore.
Your dreams
caught at the window
hang like stars.

Enough! or Too Much

Endless witless poverty.
At four below
cold is the first affirmation,
Cleaning the kitchen floor
without whys or wherefores,
we trouble the councils of the
    wise.
What do we know
brother slut, sister hole?
Love overlooked, solitude, fear.
Low sun through the window.
Kneel on the warm tiles
until you remember
every flake of snow ever.

Lullaby of the Thimble
—after Rilke

Close your eyes.
What is it?
What do you seek?
What have you lost?
Remember the girl
who lost her silver thimble?
"What are you looking for?"
an old man asked her.
She said, not far from tears,
"I am looking for God."
Taking her hand, he said,
"Just look—
what a beautiful thimble I found
    today."

The Most Sublime Act Is to Set Another Before You

It is a bitter thing,
all morning they bickered—
irritations by the bedclothes,
fault over tomorrow's spoons,
raised voices at the back door,
silence pegging the clothes
on a frozen line.

Windy day.
Just this fluttering,
blameless
as the chattering birds.

Lullaby of Death

For though our life may be
a thing to share, who is there
in this world to share our death?
—Brodsky

It's okay.
It's nothing at all.
It does not count.
Nothing has happened.
Everything remains the same.
I am I. You are you
and the old life
is unchanged, untouched.
Whatever we were
we are still.
Call me by the old familiar
    names.
Speak to me in the easy way
you always used.

In Seed-Time Learn, in Harvest Teach, in Winter Enjoy

The old fools—
whatever it was they didn't know,
I don't want to know it either.
We are told to give away
what most we want
when all the evidence
says there is nothing to gain in
    giving.

Tableware and crockery
    transformed
light streaming across the
    afternoon
absolutely taking in every
    shadow and cry
returning just this
already and always.

Lullaby of the Disappeared

Evening tills the lonely street.
September moon and the scent
of burnt food over traffic and
    trees.
Bones in a box,
blood in the alley dust,
smoke in the air.

He Who Desires but Acts Not Breeds Pestilence

Once in snowdusk by halfmoon
  light
I met one of the walking
  wounded
and he pulled hard at his wound
to see his color inside and his
  smell

saying once there was almost
  something
somehow not quite near
for instance not the words
nor even their letters spoken
nevertheless just a little way off

perhaps partially missing
or blurred at the crucial moment
already too late
or the wrong way round
or something like failure
but not really
your own end
tied around your neck.

Lullaby of the Beekeeper of Chillan

Even God sleeps now, my loves,
even failures and sin
snore alongside speech and truth,
but the bees do not sleep.

The grapes in the arbor sleep,
the old car in the back.
The lock in the gate sleeps,
the plum and cherry trees,
but the bees do not sleep.

The broom and the toilet sleep
and the old cobbles in the road.
The wife and the small grey
  birds sleep
and the bitter insect infesting the
  hive.
The door in its varnish sleeps,
but my bees do not sleep.

The stray dogs in the trash,
the wax sealed larvae sleep,
even the washing, the angels, the
  stars.
Things come and go,
but the bees do not sleep.

The Lust of the Goat Is the Bounty of God

Pinned under my tongue all
   these wishes
arrive in my sleep
leaving shadows and stars
in a summery green park
where I lecture to women
who undress themselves
hang their clothes on me
sit in comfortable chairs, relax
and look at me with curiosity.

Lullaby of Wonder

Over the old house by the fields
the wild birds are falling,
the notes of the leaves
and the air.
They come from my own breast
blessing the drawn light,
the breath, the need.
It is the way it has to be
among the families of the wind.

A Fool Sees Not the Same Tree That the Wise Man Sees

Lake snows are expected.
Birds pile up at the feeder.
The morning chores are done
    regardless.
What haunts far more than
    longing?
What is not held
when you embrace the edges?
What does it remind you of?
Grey masses pile up in the west.
Somewhere. Nowhere. What
    difference?
We put our instruments aside.
This is the end of the past,
a silent storm.
First flakes swirl
and our eyes call to them
by what name?
To know is to be someone.
To be someone is to be alone.
A little can last forever.

Lullaby of Wabi

How many days
wear the smell
from my hands?

Eternity Is in Love with the Productions of Time

How long is one?
The damaging bribes of death
disappear so that one thing,
even though all things are always
    present,
may show in the hand.

If anyone asks,
what will you say?
The old solutions dry up
and no one will explain why
there are not new ones.
You will be forgotten
over and over.

Crow weather—
black winged
picking sodden debris
in the rain.

Lullaby of Mujo

Never mind the names
sifting in a random wind.
Rain on the remains,
moss, leaves, stone.

The Hours of Folly Are Measured by the Clock but of Wisdom No Clock Can Measure

Death tells all which is nothing.
Close to the dangerous borders
you look around.
It is still there,
the clamoring of what you
      missed,
the skin of time
crumpled like roadkill,
your lists of omissions.

The granddaughter of reason
has deceived you
among the upper and lower skies,
the old house across the marshes,
the instruments and papers
scattered about the maw of the
      earth.
Even when facts are worse than
      suspicions
the suspicions are worse.

You thought you were great
because your remoteness was
      great
but now you open even as you
      die,
peddling last words for each
      moment.

You eat not because you're
      hungry
but because you're alive.
Go fight with your worms.

Lullaby of Sabi

I never knew
love was grief
and bare stone.

The Eye of Fire, the Nostrils of Air, the Mouth of Water, the Beard of Earth

There is love more quiet
even than solitude,
even than late snows
in the grey evening,
than the flickering, neighborly
   work
of shovels and plows,
that gives itself away
and returns again and goes
without ceasing and without
   alternative.
What could we say,
one who is never alone to one
   always so?
I did not mistake you for
   another.

Lullaby of Osaki-ni

Who loves the pilgrim
and the changing face,
the first look of the shadows?
Who stoops over your bed,
who eases your whimpering?
Who bears the day burdens
into evening,
who is half lost in gathering
   night?
Had we been young together
you would know
the grey wind and the stars
turn in the wake.

What's Now Proved Was Once Only Imagined

Moonslip over spring snows
poised to thaw.
Touch and grace,
the unsettled, unnumbered
   things,
woe without bounds
and the seedbed of wholeness.
Some mornings I wake without
   thanks
and am ashamed.
Even dogs,
when fed for just three days,
never forget.

Lullaby of No Duplicity

Sleep and meaning fall to shreds.
Look at your longtime
   companion.
Emptiness does not
create the many things.
It reveals them
by showing itself
as them.
Bless the empty love
without boundaries
without abiding form
wholly, only, and always.

Shame Is Pride's Cloak

Anger, greed, sorrow, pride—
just possibilities that haunt
because they are not whole;
the implications of time and
    space,
not crows and small birds in the
    morning,
not the grey wind nor the gold.

Unbodied speech and
    disappointments,
exquisite clues
to everything you use
to become unlovable.
Once again you fail.

Bow with humility, bow with
    rage.
Bow to the one
who bows before the wind.
Lift up your voice and plead
    for all.

Lullaby of Entropy

How do you pray for faith?
Wind without sound
wakes voices from other things.
Earn your way
back into being
by saying
the silence after the music.

THINK IN THE MORNING,
ACT IN THE NOON,
EAT IN THE EVENING,
SLEEP IN THE NIGHT
—*after Ficino*

And your inward sky?
It is a very subtle body
almost not a body
indeed almost your silence
or it is almost not your silence
in its power—it is less
like giving up giving up
more like water or air
or most of all
the fire of the stars
o my beginner beginning.

LULLABY OF TWO HERONS
RISING FROM STILL WATERS

It is to be with God
before he cried out.
It is to be the light.
Do not be afraid.
There are no others.

Everything Possible to Be Believed Is an Image of Truth

For the moment cars have
    stopped passing
on the main road.
Cold crackles the very air
over the whole city.
A window unlearns itself
and the full winter moon
rises over the blue
    neighborhoods.
It does not change anything.

Lullaby of the Ruined Room of Errors

Yesterday's underwear
sleeps by the foot of the bed.
The bed digs its fat legs
into the rug
dreaming of rumpled weight.
The curtains, the dust in corners,
the aches and words
that lie in shadows,
the knobs, latches,
the cat in the socks
under the bed,
the frozen ground
that holds the snoring house,
failures and fears twitching
like old dogs dreaming,
the mouse droppings and flies
caught in a lazy web
all sleep.
Nothing is wise or aware,
each at rest in itself
in the dark
without witness.

Truth Can Never Be Told so as to Be Understood and Not Be Believed

Fog seeps out of the February
    night
and yellow lamps draw windows
in on themselves.
People gather round them
and speak in muted tones
against the vast black.
Nothing can be seen.
Loneliness swirls like smoke.
Children hear things in the
    cellar,
they feel the whispers,
the grey shadows between
    thoughts,
the movement outside
just beyond the streetlamp,
the unfamiliar face gazing back
from the reflecting window
just before sleep,
the uneasy waiting
for the frenzy of the wind and
    stars.

Lullaby of Exultation's Shell

Out across the brute land
hard by the hills
Autumn deepens,
the wind blows.
The wind blows
snow in the grey air,
in the hollow space of words,
that boney place
where men hold out,
some by sleep,
some by death,
some by breath.

Lullaby of Crossing the River

Carrying a day
is like carrying a mountain,
those endless small words
men use to guard
their helplessness.
Put your day down.
Come to the bank in the snow
wearing grace and pain,
the silence at the end of sentences.
Breathe the snow
and the sad odor of human dust.
All the roads are inside you,
even the desire
not to desire
brooding over your own horizon.
The innocents await you.
There is no one to wish farewell
except yourself in the orphaned dark.

III.

WAYS TO LIVE HAPPILY

Titles for these poems are from the Venerable Eido Shimano Roshi's *Five Ways to Live Happily*.

KNOW THAT AFTER ALL
LIFE IS SIMPLE
DO NOT COMPLICATE IT

  This morning at breakfast
  as we touch our teacups together
  and listen to the news
  tell me your name again
  for I always forget.

BE GENEROUS
IN YOUR THOUGHTS, DEEDS, AND THINGS

  No one understands
  the subtle work of small grey birds—
  what will count

is the tenderness evoked
in those who come after
remembered breath, unconfused words.
All things fear not to live.
Awareness, not fear,
is our humanity.

Remember that Things Go According to Your Karma Whether You Like It or Not

One day, my dear,
you stop and look around you,
find yourself stuffing needs
into a sack of thoughts,
realize you have talked your life
to pieces,
scratched your self to bits,
that neither hope nor doubt
can protect you,
that you are not mistaken,
that you haven't lost your grip —
it is dissolving.
Now you can speak
about everything silently.

Humbly Obey the Law of the Universe

Looking up, cold spring rains
splatter over my face

and run under my collar.
Looking down, the drops splatter
into the puddle at my feet.
That tall reflection of someone
vanishes.

Be Positive under Any Circumstances

Let me say that I love you
when you lie ringed with death.
Though love cannot always find a way
out of your fear,
it is not for your life
but for your truth you are afraid.
The blessing is not that we say you are true
but that you are.

IV.

THE THREE INFINITIES

INFINITE GRATITUDE TO THE PAST

The ravaged road goes on and on
in both directions.
Who can I ask to buy the bones?

Snow settles on hemlock and yew.
This is enough
to the end of my days
without end amen.

INFINITE SERVICE TO THE PRESENT

Nothing remote
about this house in the city in the snow,
but we dwell in empty freedom nevertheless.
Snow fills the drive and walk.
Subtle endless tones of grey all day.
At dusk the sun dips
below the western cloud cover

and last lights linger
on roof ridges and trees in the east.
Silence so sweet
even the hungry ghosts listen.

Every evening birds come to roost
on the house next door.
The beautiful old maple out front
is enough to sadden you to death.
No one has been seen at a window
in a long time.
The boy is now a confused man
left unprepared for the world,
its dues, burdens, and dust.
All lost in a tax auction
after three generations.
Where will he go?

No one asks the latecomer who he is
or how he got here
and he has forgotten himself.
My need is so great, he says,
I don't care what your problems are.
He is dying from death,
turning into haze and mist,
and the pain, well,
it burns up everything
even ash.
You don't know, he says,
who you are
or where you're going,
help me.

Sometimes a whisper, sometimes a roar,
without deficiency or condition—
why are you angry
when I cannot tell you its source?
Because I am dull and tongue-tied
does not mean
the light shines less brightly.
Are there exceptions?
These games are meaningless
and the need to show you
the source of my being
fades like winter stars at dawn.
You are with me always
in what is now
the wounded place and the whole,
our breath visible in the cold air.

INFINITE RESPONSIBILITY TO THE FUTURE

What possible meaning
could birds have
flocked to an old chimney
in late afternoon
as my son takes the car
down the street and into the snow?
Without this moment
nothing else will happen.
Beloved moonsnares and foxwords
everything is incomprehensible
now and then.

V.

BLUE HEAPED UPON BLUE

WOODTHRUSH
—for Bryna

Each place is the end of the world.
This is the sound of what remains
out across long dusk,
your small fist of sleep in my hand
where a plain brown bird sounds
from the deepwood.

The tiny irreparable damage of living
is what I have given you.
By this sound be initiated
and see deeply.

Do not forget the myth of your body
for I once forgot mine
and the monk without faith
slept better than I.

Perhaps you will find what ruled me
after I am dead, for its fires
are still dark to me.

It is not skill, knowledge, intellect,
good luck or bad, but choosing
to feel the strange notes of our wildness,
for there is not nothingness
despite the easy magic of despair.

Read these woodsigns
hidden beyond the first steps
and regain our love in this sound.
Roads will never be closed to you.

We stand in a meadow of fireflies and timothy.
The sky lies pale with some stars.

BECOMING THE MOUNTAIN
—for Conor

They stood on a road in December.
Wind made snow ghosts among the trees.
The child asked, "Where does the wind come from?"

It comes from the mouth of nowhere,
between day and dark
so the trees can talk together.

"But it's winter now
and the trees are sleeping."

Yes, so listen carefully
to their dreams.

"And suppose I am the wind?"

Then you are also the dreams.

SWEET TIMOTHY
—*for Jane on our 25th*

I
(1970–72)

White are the beds of April,
waylaid beautiful fire
burning out of luck and life,
being earlier than I have ever thought,
where, once leaves breathe
in the walk of morning,
light flakes green.

Children are the first awake,
before milk or bird,
waiting for sound
and the secret bowers of summer.
Wind through sunlight.
Cobwebs on the rhubarb leaves.
What flows between me but
even spring,
even water
drying inward from the edges.

Sweet timothy of days and my dear
tell me many times
how hot are the beds of summer.
Say at last a bush is burning,
lovely as life
when the thought is on us,
hatched in loitering acts
and rising all the time,
though there is time enough
to die in life as lovely as aching;
or being found out in my prayer,
leave me half on fire,
throwing off attitudes like flame,
for these grave eyes divine what
but that there is not in being one
I may love after you.

II
(1994)

These uncertain hands
carry both love and poison,
have been our undoing many times,
but refuse to disappear.
Take them again—
recall their stubborn particulars
as we return to the bluegreen meadow
wholly dependent on our inabilities.
Goldfinch, redwing, the hawk-stunned air,
the endlessly uttering grasses
say still there breathes no other
across a thousand miles of evening.

VI.

A BOY RUNNING IN THE WIND

St. Nadie's Canticle of Ecstasy

On a winter day at a certain time,
perhaps at the edge of spring,
what is the voice of this stone,
this trashcan rolling in the wind,
clustered snowdrops bending?
Listening, listening,
a woman stands in the sunny March winds,
sudden snowflakes flying, sudden sun.
I have to tell you
my joy is not care free.
It is full of cares
and the wild careless blowing manyweathers,
crows, shadows, winds.

Days full of time, days empty.
Dust and fumes follow the buses,
always one shoe by the side,
seven crows over the wood,

standing corn broken in the field.
Trust yourself and the unfolding circumstances.

Longer days, shorter shadows,
all the lost minutes, the turn of water,
ducks still homing
to the dead stream.
Trust is different from acceptance.

By the window, blue evening
turning dark.
Stars, cars, lights going someplace else.
A dog barks in another neighborhood,
uncertainty and cold,
waning moon so clear
eyes blur with tears.

Whatever you think will be lost
remains to be discovered endlessly.
I know I will die, still,
another day of life—what luck!
Noise and distress, stars and emptiness,
coyotes on a wooded hill.
Where does the city end?
Inside, they lick the bowl together,
father and son.

Who is this? Pools after rain,
bare trees, birds roosting.
If I reach today by exile
the road behind
is a windblown meadow.

Work slowly
as a crabapple bud.
Only the happiness of others
tastes like this,
my face with the trees
against the sky.

Moss, green rock breath;
sky, road, spring winds;
rainy day, sunny day, same day;
day and night trees stand,
old bark wrinkling,
rain, bird, single breath.

Boughs beat against the house,
more unexpected snows
and a slant of light;
burning leaves,
all the children of the world
dance round,
finitude with each endless step.

I will die, I will laugh.
Look who comes near: the dead, the stars,
tomorrow's sky, today's field,
a silent house.
How many deaths in this town today
under windy blue?

Crows, chickadees, small grey birds
ply their being;
weeds, rubbish, people,
wondrous whiles.

I spoiled your departure my beloveds.
You leave silently, even unnoticed,
but I breathe you back
into the room,
into the faint strings of stars.

What I wish for my son
(rain, peace, love, wind)
I wish for you.
I wish you the beautiful sun
that gets shady sometimes
in the wind I love like a lover
for you will leave me forever
before you return.

All the tides, all the winds,
all the sorrows, all the songs—
we have everything we need.
Each day the amazing crows are black.
Wind never picks up anything
to put it away.
Sun, crows, shadows,
my common paradise;
tree trunks sun warming,
slow in the wind.
I've lived, am older,
the sweetness of crows flying away,
maybe the only man satisfied with morning,
cloud, light, bluster—
a boy running in the wind.

St. Nadie and the Gracehoper

—for Reggie

Just when I think I am alone
singing among the stars
you turn up, my beloved,
and my tears of thought
turn into matter.

Hey, no problem, brother!
The whole day is gratis.
You can take your airy processes
to the great somebody somewhere
and ring his paunch.
Having said that,
waste not with want
any extra beforeness
in the name of the former
and of the latter.

I give you
the irrational, unearned
winter morning.

You can't give me nothing.

SHE TELLS HIM HOW NOW SHE IS REARRANGED

This sadness, tears, this vulnerability
                are shock waves of the hurt.
What was my hurt?

I still look around me
                in every direction.
What is my fear?

I dream that everywhere I go
        there is no one to support me.
What is my need?

Who am I when November winds
                spread over the grey hills
sing in my nest of bones?

Who is it trails my hand
                from the drifting canoe
in north lake waters?

I am the answer and the water
                and the wind.

The Thieves Roar Like Fish in the Sand

There are demons
in the endless wood.
No one believes in them
but they are there
to sizzle like poisoned water
in the heart.

Twigs crack in the wind.
We fumble the tools,
our tongues stutter.

Light is a danger.
With it we see only
to the edge of it.

Now the owl speaks out.
Snow falls regardless and slow.

Time and making in time are made.
Lying together in the morning,
caught by expectations,
caught by snow flickering
on glass without edges,
we see only faceless grey light.
Once without a name ever so,
the wild unmade stars alive
in our upturned faces.

Habit of Being

When I took that first step
between the wind
I still felt your thoughts
floating through mine.

When by force of mediocrity
I grasped at grasping hope
and became the usual
self-referencing awareness
you were rain
in a hundred different places.

When I applied the fatalities
which rule us
you were air behind rushing cars
spinning the dust and litter
like flowers in the morning.

When I took the icons from the pavilion
to the plains of appetite
you were budding trees in playgrounds
of abandoned schools.

When I was unprepared for
the night
you were night sounds
free of all hearers
and my gift to you was my fallacy.

When it was a case of silence
we still listened

but when it was blindness
I was no longer looking.

When now I am you
each apprehension aspires
to blue breath of speedwell in the grasses
and the light song
of a whitethroated sparrow.

FROM CAMBIOS

CXXV

We gave up sainthood and wisdom
to know our place, to burn a little, to be still
and so master the restless wind.
It comes from fire,
a sign of mystery
and a sign of the family.
It merges with dust
to become visible.

CXXV *Chia Jen* (family, clan)

CCLXXXVIII

Constellations are stillness,
the miscellaneous distance of stars
racing away, the lie of light,

one form of sight.
Who contemplates the forms,
the shapes, the changes of time
or perhaps the forms of men
holding hard to bony ways,
the world thought of,
has also the sense
without an explanation of it.

CCLXXXVIII *Pi* (grace)

A MERCIFUL AVATAR FARTS IN THE ZENDO

This truth,
incomparably profound and minutely subtle,
is hardly met with
even in hundreds of thousands of millions of eons.
No thought, no volition,
no consciousness, no suffering.
If we listen to this truth
and praise it
and gladly embrace it
we have really gone beyond foolish talk.
We now can see this,
listen to this,
accept and hold this.
As the truth eternally reveals itself
at this moment
what more need we seek?
How transparent the perfect moonlight.
How boundless the cleared sky.
The gate of oneness
of cause and effect is opened.

VII.

AN ENDLESS VOW

SOEN'S DRAGON

There are some things we know
before we had words to tell us
we knew them.
We are fastened to them
though they are not fastened to us.

Remember once April hills held the snow
and field stones were warm in the sun.
I basked like an old dog
and found a newt dead by my foot.
It's with me now.
The eye sockets are empty.
There is nothing inside.

How did the body survive the winter?
How did it escape
the birds and small animals
to die there,

dry, perfect in each detail,
whole down to the last brown toe?

As we clutch and breathe
the smoke of sublimation
I hold this light of emptiness
in my hand.

On Becoming a Monk

No one behind. No one ahead.
Just this place and point.
All escape routes end here
and the maps proved useless long ago.
The thousand disguises are in tatters
along the road behind.
Out here, vast emptiness—
the life-cries of the world's lost billions.

Just these guides
in the containing silence:
a thrush at dusk, a star at dawn.

Who puts his foot down again in the dust?
Whose foot again and again, ceaselessly?

BOWING
—*for Shinge Roshi and the sangha of Hoen-ji*

In this empty house
I have thrown
all the windows open for you.
Upstairs in the irreligious dark
nothing remains
to whisper as you approach.
Come, play here now,
each in your shimmering exactitude—
spring rains, flowering lilacs,
countless birdsongs.

MOST INTIMATE

How wonderful, how blessed!
Is this one, is this two?
—Mumonkan, case 35

Playing alone in the dirt,
he smells the tiniest grain
as a few small toys push along.

Foxgrape ablaze in cedars
above him, behind him.
He knows their red.

So silent, the sparrows stand
on the rock just by him.
He feels the quick sidelong glance.

Late and slow in the cold
a bee touches blue chicory.
He hears the patient work

Sun flash, October shadows
on his neck and hair.
He sees them. His hand moves.

Same day each sky.
New winds, this boy.
Not once does he wonder.
No one in the sky in his heart.

NOTHING TO PROVE

Who sees me by form,
who seeks me in sound,
wrongly turned
are his footsteps on the Way.
—Diamond Sutra, verse 26

We come to spring
both the stakes and the gambler,
putting our lives on the table
as if life were ours.
The light of suspicion in our eyes
recalls our own faithless breaths.
Swayed by words
we wander the wind
bewildered, looking for evidence
of something not quite there,
a face—proof we are not alone.

You are not alone my beloveds.
You cannot be alone.
There is no such thing as alone.
You are the air I breathe
and I am your very breath.
Because of you
I cannot be sad in this world.
And what with breakdowns and so on
who would say it hasn't been hard going?
Do you look up at Death there
by the roadside
jingling chips of your fate
in his pockets,
watching us under the cutting north wind,
the brilliant moon, the wild white clouds,
not so much there as beside the point?
And if you ask whether I regret starting out
my voice rises like flocks of finches at dawn
and blows across the deep blue sky.

ABOUT THE AUTHOR

 TERRANCE KEENAN is an Irish artist, writer and
Zen Buddhist monk. He was formerly a university
lecturer, independent bookseller, special collections
librarian, and performed many of the duties and roles
of head monk at the Zen Center of Syracuse. His
poetry, essays, and reviews have appeared in national
journals in the United States and in numerous anthologies. He has
published four books of poems. Syracuse University Press published
If Our Lives Be Spared, his iconoclastic history covering 170 years of an
American family that settled the New York State wilderness in 1816.
He was ordained in 1994 by Shinge-shitsu Roko Sherry Chayat Roshi,
abbot of the Zen Center of Syracuse Hoen-ji and Dai Bosatsu Zendo
Kongo-ji. He lives with his wife in West Cork, Ireland.

ABOUT WISDOM PUBLICATIONS

Wisdom Publications is the leading publisher of contemporary and classic Buddhist books and practical works on mindfulness. Publishing books from all major Buddhist traditions, Wisdom is a nonprofit charitable organization dedicated to cultivating Buddhist voices the world over, advancing critical scholarship, and preserving and sharing Buddhist literary culture.

To learn more about us or to explore our other books, please visit our website at www.wisdompubs.org. You can subscribe to our eNewsletter, request a print catalog, and find out how you can help support Wisdom's mission either online or by writing to:

Wisdom Publications
199 Elm Street
Somerville, Massachusetts 02144 USA

You can also contact us at 617-776-7416 or info@wisdompubs.org.

Wisdom is a 501(c)(3) organization, and donations in support of our mission are tax deductible.

Wisdom Publications is affiliated with the Foundation for the Preservation of the Mahayana Tradition (FPMT).